CASHFLOW AND CREDIT MANAGEMENT

The Daily Telegraph
ESSENTIAL MANAGEMENT TECHNIQUES

CASHFLOW AND CREDIT MANAGEMENT

VALERIE HAWKES & KEN SLATER
PEAT MARWICK McLINTOCK
MANAGEMENT CONSULTANTS

Published by Telegraph Publications
Peterborough Court, At South Quay,
181 Marsh Wall, London E14 9SR

Series Editor: Marlene Garsia

Typeset by Bookworm Typesetting, Manchester

Printed in Great Britain by Biddles Ltd,
Guildford and King's Lynn

British Library Cataloguing in Publication Data

Hawkes, Valerie
  Cash flow and credit management.—
  (Essential management techniques).
  1. Cash flow
  I. Title II. Slater, Ken III. Series
  658.1'5244   HG4028.C45

  ISBN 0–86367–226–4

Contents

Introduction

The aim of this book is to provide a practical examination of cashflow and credit management for middle managers within businesses, both medium-sized companies and small firms.

The emphasis is on illustration and example throughout, with the book guiding managers into new areas of cash management and offering new ideas on familiar topics. This is not a theoretical textbook to gather dust on the office shelf; it is a handbook to be used at work.

Cashflow and Credit Management describes the basis of each subject area before moving on to deal with more complex issues. This makes the work accessible to both the financial and the non-financial manager within the business. Since your fundamental requirement will be to translate the practices described into your office, we have continuously borne in mind the vital question: 'How can this work for me?'

This book addresses all the major cash and credit-management issues which face businesses operating in the UK. However, within the constraints of one volume, it has not been possible to cover all topics in equal depth. Our approach to this dilemma has therefore been to tackle the most fundamental issues in the greatest detail, and to give less consideration to more peripheral topics such as 'money-market dealing' and 'foreign-trade management'. This is not to imply that certain topics have less importance to the business than others, merely that their inclusion in a book on cash management is more questionable. This approach reflects our belief that there must be effective management of the basic areas of cash management before the more complex issues can be addressed. Or, put more simply: 'You have to walk before you can run!'

The Need for Cashflow and Credit Management

A business can be defined as a commercial firm or enterprise engaged in the activity of buying and selling goods or services. If it wishes to survive and prosper in today's economic environment it must pay close attention to all the factors which affect its cashflow.

Cashflow and credit management, in its broadest sense, relates to the planning, monitoring and controlling of factors affecting the rate and amount of cash that flows in and out of a business. The amount of cash available to a business depends on its trading performance, balance-sheet control, capital expenditure, dividend policy and the amount of borrowing and capital available. The rate of cashflow depends on the efficiency with which the business manages its stocks, debtors and creditors.

Cash, together with stocks, debtors and creditors makes up a business' working capital. Figure 1 shows the relationship between working capital, which is inherently short term, and funding, which consists of amounts invested by the owners of a

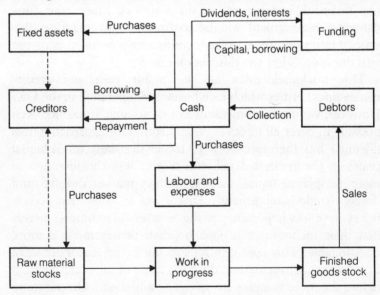

Figure 1 *Capital cycle of a business*

business (equity capital) and long-term borrowings. Equity capital and long-term borrowings are needed to finance purchases of fixed assets, such as buildings and equipment, and to finance those parts of working capital (stocks and debtors) which cannot be financed through taking credit from suppliers.

Cash flows into a business through the receipt of amounts due from customers for goods sold or services provided. It flows out of a business through wages, the purchase of raw materials and payment for overheads, such as rent, rates, power and water, and a host of other items including office equipment and stationery.

Unless a business manages its stock, keeping it as low as possible, it will have to borrow excessive sums of money to finance the investment in stock. It must, however, have sufficient stocks to satisfy demand or customers will go elsewhere for their requirements. Similarly, most businesses have to extend credit to their customers in order to generate sales. Money tied up in amounts due, or debtors, also needs to be financed, and at a cost. Purchases on credit also have to be managed. If a business takes too long to pay its suppliers it can suffer from poor supplier relations, which can generate a bad reputation and consequently lead to suppliers refusing to supply goods or grant credit.

Working capital management is critical to a business' success. Without sufficient cash a business will be unable to meet its commitments and will be forced into liquidation. However, once a business receives cash it is equally important to manage it as efficiently as possible. Excess cash should be invested and cash shortages funded from short or long-term sources as appropriate. Successful businesses regularly prepare and update cashflow forecasts to enable them to anticipate and manage their working capital requirements effectively.

Many businesses trade with customers and suppliers overseas. Such activity brings with it complications not associated with the domestic market. Businesses will become involved in currency transactions and the management of exchange-rate risk, as well as facing additional contractual difficulties and commercial risks.

1

Cash Collection

Good cash collection procedures can make the difference between a profitable business and one forced into liquidation because of slow payment and default on outstanding debts.

When a business grants credit to a customer it immediately incurs two types of cost. First, there is interest. This is either paid by the business on its overdraft or other borrowings or, if the business is in the fortunate position of not owing money, is the interest which could have been earned had cash been received from the customer and invested (known as 'opportunity cost'). Second, there is cost in the administration of outstanding debts, in terms of both the people and the systems involved in the collection process.

The key features of a good cash collection cycle are:
- Proper internal control procedures.
- Fast conversion of stocks to debtors to cash.
- Minimisation of costs.

These factors are considered under each of the various stages of cash collection, as follows.

- Evaluating credit-worthiness of customers.
- Setting credit limits.
- Defining terms of payment.
- Determining invoicing procedures.
- Recording and reporting amounts due.
- Collecting amounts due.

The final section in this chapter describes the structure,

organisation and training required for administering the collection of cash.

Creditworthiness of Customers

Before giving a potential customer credit, an assessment should be made ascertaining the risk of non-payment. Equally, established customers should also be monitored, as business conditions are subject to constant change.

Various sources of information exist which enable a judgement to be made of the creditworthiness of a prospective customer. The basic suggested requirements when checking a customer's status are a bank and two trade references.

Bank reference. To obtain a reference from a prospective customer's bankers it is customary to route the request through the business' own bank. The process may be speeded up by writing directly to the customer's bank requesting that a reply is given to the business' bank.

The reference request should be as precise as possible and be in the following format:

Example 1 *Bank reference request*

Dear Sirs,

XYZ Ltd.

The above-named firm have requested credit facilities from us. Will you please advise if you consider them good for trade credit up to £.... on net monthly terms.

Their bank is:

Yours faithfully,

The reply should be scrutinised carefully to ascertain its true meaning. Bankers use terms which may not have an obvious meaning due to confidentiality requirements. The advice of the supplier's banker may be sought to decipher the real meaning of the reference.

Trade references. Care should be exercised when taking up trade references because companies are unlikely to provide the names of referees who will not give a favourable report. Also, note that the prospective customer is likely to have contacted the referees advising them to expect a reference.

Example 2 *Application for credit account*

Name of company:
Address:
Telephone number:
Directors/proprietors:
Maximum credit required £ per month:
Banker's name and address:

First trade reference
Name and address:

Second trade reference
Name and address:
Please enclose a copy of letterhead for record purposes
Date:
Signature:

The request to open a credit account should normally be made in writing by the customer, and should contain the details shown in Example 2. A standard form should be made available by the supplier. It is important to get the correct name and address of the customer which may be needed when taking action over delayed payment, and the request for a letterhead is a simple means of ensuring this.

Once the supplier has received the request to open a credit account, the referees should be contacted. A letter requesting a reference, as illustrated in Example 3 should be brief, factual and confidential. As an alternative to writing to a referee the process can be speeded up by telephoning. An advantage of this method is that people are normally willing to give more information over the telephone than in a letter.

Credit-reporting agencies. A number of agencies exist in the UK providing either or both credit-rating registers and reports on particular companies. Well-known agencies include Dun and Bradstreet, CCN Systems Ltd and Infolink.

The Dun and Bradstreet Register is by far the most widely used in the UK as it details essential information on over 200,000 companies. Its use is mainly in providing a quick indication of the credit rating of the customer in question. However, as a business' standing can quickly change, and because registers can be up to two-years-old, not too much reliance should be placed on this information source.

Example 3 *Trade reference request*

Dear Sirs,
XYZ Ltd.
The above-named firm wishes to open an account with us and have given your company as a trade reference. We shall be grateful if you will answer, in confidence, the following six questions and return this letter to us in the prepaid envelope provided.

1. How long have you known XYZ Ltd?
2. How much credit do you normally allow?
3. What are your payment terms?
4. What is their highest recent payment?
5. Do they pay to your satisfaction?
6. Any further information?

We thank you in anticipation for your prompt attention to this matter.
    Yours faithfully,

Credit-reporting agencies may cover all business sectors or may specialise in only a few industries. Their value lies in providing a quick assessment of a potential customer; note however, that the services provided by agencies do vary, as does the cost.

Sales reports. The salesman is often the initiator of new business which gives rise to the need to assess the customer's credit-worthiness. A salesman, however, is normally more interested in generating sales than in helping the credit-control department to assess credit risks. However, many companies require the salesman to complete a standard form, detailing information on new and existing customers, which is used to assist in credit control.

When the credit-risk assessment is directed at an existing customer, perhaps because the customer wishes to increase his credit limit, the obvious starting point should be an analysis of his track record. A well-organised business should be able to look at a customer history on its sales ledger. This would show whether the customer regularly trades with the business and promptly settles the account.

Credit visits. In certain cases, particularly when assessing a potentially valuable customer, it is useful if he can attend a meeting with the Credit and Sales Managers. This has two benefits. One, to provide an outsider's view on how well the business is run, which could yield vital information. And second, to establish more intimate business relations.

Analysis of company accounts

Public and private limited companies have to file accounts with the Registrar of Companies. The published accounts of a company are a source of considerably detailed, if historical information, which can be useful in assessing credit risks. Information given to the Registrar of Companies includes a profit and loss account, balance sheet, the name of directors and their other directorships, a list of the company's shareholders and charges on company assets. The Companies Registry is located at Cardiff with a branch office in London.

An analysis of a prospective customer's accounts, published or otherwise, can provide useful information to aid credit-risk assessment. However, even audited accounts have limitations, which must be considered when used for credit-risk assessment.

The four drawbacks are:

1. They are based on historical information and are out of date by the time they are published. The latest accounts available at the Registrar of Companies may be over 18 months old.

2. A balance sheet is a statement of a company's assets and liabilities at a point in time, that is, on a particular day in the year. It may include distortions due to a cyclical or seasonal trading pattern.

3. It has been known for some businesses to 'window dress' their balance sheets to show a more favourable position. This is more likely where the accounts are unaudited but some measures are legitimate, for example, reducing stock levels through discounting and promotions just prior to the year end.

4. Distortions in the balance sheet arising through intercompany trading and 'off-balance sheet' financing methods, such as leasing.

When analysing published accounts one of the first things to look at is the auditor's report. Any material qualification should be noted. The notes to the accounts should be scrutinised to find out if other creditors have prior charges on the business' assets.

A very useful tool for the analysis of accounts is the use of ratios. Meaningful analysis involves comparing trends in the same ratio over time, and in comparing ratios against the industry norm or average. It is possible to calculate and compare many different ratios which have varying degrees of usefulness, depending on the business in question. The most important types of ratios for credit-risk assessment can be classified as either liquidity or profitability related.

The liquid ratio, often referred to as the acid test or quick ratio, is a very good indicator of a business' ability to meet its immediate commitments. This ratio is calculated as follows:

$$\frac{\text{Liquid assets}}{\text{Current liabilities}} \quad \text{which is} \quad \frac{\text{Cash, debtors and securities}}{\text{Trade creditors} + \text{short-term liabilities}}$$

A ratio of 1:1 indicates good liquidity because it implies that the business could meet its immediate debts from short-term funds. However, ratios less than this may not necessarily cause concern if they are in line with the industry standard. Any ratio below 0.5:1 should be seen as a danger signal.

The current or working-capital ratio gives a measure of working capital available at a given time and is calculated as:

$$\frac{\text{Current assets}}{\text{Current liabilities}}$$

A crude rule of thumb is that this ratio should be 2:1 to indicate good liquidity. It needs to be higher than the liquid ratio as the current assets figure used includes stocks, which may not be quickly realisable into cash. However, the ratio can be misleading because conditions vary so much from one business to another, and from time to time. Factors including seasonal sales, asset purchases, order book, length of production cycle, credit period granted by creditors and so on influence the norm for this ratio. Again, trends and industry norms are appropriate bench marks.

A business needs to be profitable and have a positive cashflow to survive in the long term. So when analysing accounts look at the trend in profits over a period. A declining trend is an obvious sign for concern.

The primary ratio for profitability measurement is return on capital employed, calculated as:

$$\frac{\text{Net profit}}{\text{Capital employed}}$$

This primary ratio can be further analysed into two secondary ratios:

$$\frac{\text{Net profit}}{\text{Turnover}} \quad \text{and} \quad \frac{\text{Turnover}}{\text{Capital employed}}$$

Capital employed includes share capital, reserves and undistributed profits.

As well as the absolute magnitude of profits, it is necessary to relate profits to both sales and capital employed to see whether an adequate return has been made. Investors would be happy with, for example, £100,000 profit on capital employed of £750,000 which is a return of 13.3 per cent. However, only a 1 per cent return would be achieved on £10 million capital, which would be considered inadequate.

It must be emphasised that these ratios are only useful when compared over a period of time and with similar businesses. Other ratios can help give an insight into a business' efficiency and organisation, six of which are detailed below.

1. Debt-collection period $= \dfrac{\text{Trade debtors}}{\text{Average daily turnover}}$

shows efficiency of credit control, and indicates the likelihood of debtors providing cash to pay for goods which the business has bought on credit.

2. Bad-debt ratio $= \dfrac{\text{Bad debts incurred}}{\text{Total turnover on credit}}$

3. Number of days of finished stock $=$
$$\dfrac{\text{Value of finished stock}}{\text{Average daily cost of sales}}$$
showing how quickly stocks are converted into sales.

4. Number of days of raw material stock $=$
$$\dfrac{\text{Value of raw materials stock}}{\text{Average daily use of raw materials}}$$

5. Credit payment period $= \dfrac{\text{Trade creditors}}{\text{Average daily purchases}}$
showing how quickly suppliers are paid.

6. Gearing ratio $= \dfrac{\text{Long-term debt + preference shares}}{\text{Ordinary shareholders funds}}$
showing how much debt exists compared to equity. A high-

geared company runs the risk of running into liquidity problems as interest has to be paid whether or not the company is earning profits.

Credit Limits

Once a prospective customer's creditworthiness has been analysed and his request for credit agreed, the credit limit must now be set. This is the total amount a business will supply a customer without cash payment. If the limit requested appears unjustifiably high, or if some doubt exists as to the customer's ability or intention to pay, a lower limit could initially be set.

Credit limits should be monitored over a period of time. Customers who reliably trade near their limit may prove to be a source of increased turnover if the limit is increased. Where limits are exceeded a decision must be taken whether to insist on payment before delivery. This is a question of judgement which can only be made in light of the known facts.

Credit limits should be communicated to customers to avoid potential problems with refused or delayed-order processing. Equally important is the need to communicate credit limits to salesmen to avoid the embarrassment of hard-earned orders being rejected due to their being outside agreed limits.

Risk categories

In order to aid the monitoring of customer accounts, it is useful to categorise customers according to the likely risk of their defaulting on payment. It is common to place customers with a low-credit risk, such as government bodies and large 'blue chip' companies, in category 'A'. At the other extreme, category 'D', are customers of doubtful standing with poor-payment records. Categories 'B' and 'C' are reserved for intermediate risk classes. Having categorised customers according to their risk class the business can concentrate its attentions on those in the higher risk classes.

Terms of Payment

Terms of payment refers to the credit term offered by a business to its customers. The selection and negotiation of terms of payment are of great importance as they determine the planned rate of cashflow into a business from sales of goods or services.

Credit policy is an essential element in a business' marketing strategy. Given the need to balance increased profitability through increasing credit sales, with the risk of default or slow payment, good credit management is essential to the success of a business.

It is important to recognise that one factor in the successful marketing of a product is the terms of credit. In some cases, a debt-collection period that is longer than the industry norm would be acceptable. A business should regularly review its credit policy to ensure it is set to maximise sales within risk and liquidity constraints. Also, from time to time, a customer may have a particular payment problem when it will be necessary to consider all the circumstances, as well as possible future orders, in deciding upon the best course of action.

Types of credit terms

A large number of credit terms can be used. The 10 most common are:

1. *Net monthly.* The settlement for one month's deliveries, or one month's invoices, is due at (or before) the end of the following month. These terms are often subject to abuse as customers frequently exclude the last week's invoices from their bought ledger payment run. The excuse often given, perhaps genuinely, is that the computerised accounting system has to be cut off by a certain date. The effect is that the customer receives up to 38 days' extra credit.

2. *Net 30 days.* Strictly applied this term means that each day's invoices should be settled within 30 days. This gives an average 15 days faster payment than net monthly. The same principles apply to 7, 14, 21 or any other number of days as apply to net 30 days. The shorter the period the tighter the control and the smaller the risk of slow or non payment.

3. *Settlement by 21st of the following month,* that is, due by 21st of the month following the date of the invoice. These terms are relatively new and are used mainly by large businesses. Their advantage is that accounts not paid by this date can be chased with the aim of ensuring collection by the end of the month.

4. *Stage or progress payments.* These are common where there is a long delivery period or long manufacturing time with a large capital outlay, for example, building industry or machine tools. It is usual for a supplier to request a down payment before commencing manufacture (10–30 per cent is usual) with the balance being paid on completion or at agreed stages of completion or manufacture. The amounts of stage payments usually relate to the length of the manufacturing period and the cost of raw materials involved.

5. *Cash with order.* These are the harshest terms of all as no work or selection of goods or services will be provided until payment arrives. In extreme cases, where the investigation into the customer's creditworthiness reveals something untoward, it is prudent to insist on pro forma invoices being paid prior to despatch of goods. This is also the most suitable basis for dealing with a prospective credit customer while checks are being carried out.

6. *Cash before shipment,* which is marginally less harsh than cash with order.

7. *Cash on delivery.* There is some risk with cash on delivery (COD) if the goods are not accepted, or if the cheque given to the deliverer is dishonoured.

8. *Load over load.* Payment of the previous delivery is made before the current load is handed over. These terms are used when regular deliveries are involved, for example in petrol and fuel oil businesses.

9. *Discounts.* Here the terms offer the customer a discount for paying within an agreed period which is less than the normal credit period offered. Cash discounts are becoming less frequent and are usually only used where it is customary within the trade.

Discounts can be very costly indeed. For example, if a 2½ per cent cash discount is given because a customer pays one month earlier than normal, that is equivalent to interest at the rate of 30 per cent per annum. Unless the supplier's cost of borrowing was more than 30 per cent it would be uneconomic for him to offer this level of discount.

Discounts tend to cause problems because some customers will pay late and still take the discount. Also, to overcome loss of VAT, it is necessary to send out invoices net of discount. If they were sent out gross and the customer subsequently deducted the discount the supplier would lose the VAT on the discount.

However, discounts can be a valuable marketing tool when used wisely. They are suitable for high-risk perishable goods, for increasing sales where they are applied to high risk customers, and for increasing sales through the provision of a service not offered by competitors.

10. *Interest on overdue accounts.* It is possible to include, within the terms of sale, a clause enabling interest to be charged on overdue accounts. However, enforcing this clause is difficult in practice and can lead to adverse customer relations.

Selection of credit terms

The credit-worthiness of the customer is an important indication of the credit terms which should be offered to him. In addition, the business has to consider a number of other factors before deciding on which terms or combination of terms to offer its customers.

They are:

Normal trade practice. It is usual to offer the same terms as competitors unless the business has a competitive advantage, such as a reputation for superior quality. In such cases the business may be able to dictate more favourable terms due to its stronger market position.

Nature of the product. Fast-moving consumer goods, particularly food or other perishable items, are normally sold on relatively short terms compared to heavy equipment, such as a machine tool.

Size of the order. Many businesses commonly insist upon a minimum-order value before granting credit. This is particularly true of a business selling a high volume of products with a low profit margin. If credit is given where only one or a few items are purchased, the cost of administering the collection of the debt, plus the interest cost of financing the debt may make the sale uneconomic. The use of minimum-order values reduces this risk.

Financial position. If a business does not have the cash available, or access to borrowing at acceptable rates of interest, it should not offer extended credit terms.

Location of customer. A customer who is located thousands of miles away is unlikely to be logistically capable of paying within a short period, so terms such as net seven days are inappropriate.

Methods of payment

Unless the terms of payment are cash with order some credit is always given from the time goods are taken out of stock, through production and delivery, until 'value is received'. The time taken for the latter depends on the method of payment. The method of payment also has implications for cost and for ensuring that value has been received. Some of the payment methods detailed below are also considered in Chapter 7.

Cash. Consisting of notes and coins, this form of payment is required where the customer is not known or trusted. It is commonly found where low-price, low-profit margin goods are sold. In many retail businesses it is the only acceptable form of payment.

Cheques. The usual form of payment of a trade account is by cheque. With this method of payment the credit period extends to the date the cheque is cleared, which is usually three working days after it has been banked. Where the customer's financial position is satisfactory, but doubt exists as to whether he will keep to the supplier's payment terms, then a post-dated cheque received on delivery may be required. In other circumstances post-dated cheques should not be accepted as they indicate a potential problem in receiving payment. Cheques can be specially cleared by the bank if the business wishes to reduce the cheque clearance period.

Bankers drafts. These are cheques issued by the bank whose name it bears. They are often required in settlement of high-value transactions, such as vehicle or land sales, or where the financial standing of the customer is suspect.

Bankers transfers. These are fairly common in the UK but more so on the Continent. The advantage to the customer is in reduced administrative time and cost, including those related to the signing of cheques.

Promissory note. This instrument is similar to a post-dated cheque because it constitutes a promise to pay a certain sum on a certain date. Its main value is in providing proof of debt; it is usually found where large transactions are concerned.

Bills of exchange. A bill is an unconditional promise to pay the amount stated on a given date. The bill of exchange has to be accepted for payment by the customer and is payable to the supplier. Endorsed bills (usually endorsed by a financial institution, particularly Accepting Houses) are very negotiable and are commonly found in export trade.

Direct debits. Where possible a supplier should get his customer to agree to his bank account being directly debited on a certain date each month. The supplier presents a direct-debit authority, signed by his customer, to the customer's bank. The bank then transfers the appropriate amount when due. Direct debits can be stopped by a customer at any time before payment has left his bank account.

Contra accounts. Where a customer also supplies goods or services it is possible to set-off balances on the accounts and only pay the net amount. Contra accounts present problems which has led to their becoming unpopular, the main drawbacks concerning disputed items and disagreement with balances, particularly where the customer and supplier have different cut-off dates. However, contra accounts are useful if it is difficult to get payment by other means.

Invoicing Procedures

Invoicing procedures cover a business' internal procedures from the time an order is received, up to the moment an invoice is despatched to the customer. By ensuring that a complete, clear and accurate invoice is prepared and sent as quickly as possible to the customer, the business can greatly reduce delays in the collection cycle.

Receipt of orders

To enable goods and invoices to be despatched promptly it is important that the order is recorded accurately and transmitted rapidly for processing. Orders taken by salesmen should be transmitted frequently to ensure that credit approval and other processing steps do not delay satisfying customer requirements. Depending on the nature and size of the business, the order could be transmitted by telephone, post or even by remote entry into the company's computer system, via a terminal in the salesman's home.

Credit approval

Internal procedures should ensure that only orders which meet the business' credit policy are processed. Both the customer's creditworthiness and the agreed credit limit should have already been ascertained. It is essential to monitor each customer order to see that it meets the agreed requirements regarding size, credit terms, price-breaks or any other predetermined condition.

The order monitoring system would normally allow easy access to the current status of each customer's account. Depending upon the size of the business this could be a manual card system, a batch-based, computer-generated exception report, or a real-time computer system, accessed by a VDU. Whatever system is used it is imperative that goods are not despatched or production commenced for any order before credit has been approved.

Invoicing systems

There are two types of invoicing systems, pre-invoicing and post-invoicing.

Pre-invoicing systems are driven by the order or order-confirmation document. Invoices are sent on the day that orders are despatched but there is a risk of errors due to stock shortages or mistakes in selecting the correct goods. These types of system are most useful when products are manufactured to order and are commonly found in the heavy-engineering industry.

Post-invoicing systems usually rely on delivery confirmation or stock selection (picking) lists and are found where high-volume, low-value sales are made to a large customer base. Differences between goods ordered and delivered are minimised and invoice disputes, which lead to slow payment by customers, are therefore reduced. Where invoice production generates stock adjustments and accounts receivable entries, as is common with integrated computerised systems, post-invoicing is far more satisfactory as records are adjusted to reflect only the goods shipped.

Delays in invoicing must be kept to a minimum. Usually a

supplier will take the start of his credit period as the invoice date, or the date of invoice receipt, and not the date of receipt of the goods or services. Some delays in invoicing can be avoided by ensuring that:

- Invoices can be issued as soon as the appropriate documentation is received by the sales ledger department, and not only at the end of the month.
- Invoices do not have to be authorised or raised by personnel who may be out of the office, without providing appropriate deputies.
- Prices for goods or services are agreed and calculated on a timely basis.

Invoices should show clearly what is being invoiced and should refer to the order number. They should be accurately priced to minimise customer queries. Invoices should be distinctive in design, colour and format so that the customer can distinguish them from those of other suppliers. Wording should be clear and explicit. Even more care is necessary when trading in more than one country as terminology is interpreted differently. Payment deadlines should be stated on the invoice.

Invoices should ideally be despatched on the same date as the goods. The invoice date should be the same as the despatch date as some account-payable clerks will calculate due-by dates from the invoice date. To further minimise delays invoices should be sent out by first-class mail. It is important that they are properly addressed, using window envelopes to reduce delays and errors.

Recording and Reporting Amounts Due

The control of debtors requires accurate records from which regular reports should be produced to highlight areas requiring corrective action.

Recording

The primary source of information used in the control of

amounts due, or debtors, is the sales ledger. The basic transactions recorded on the ledger are sales, payments from customers, credit notes issued for returned goods and any other adjustments made to a customer's account. It is a detailed record of debtors' individual accounts and transactions. Invoices, credit notes and payments received should be entered onto this ledger on a daily basis to provide up-to-date information for credit-control purposes.

Microcomputers have fallen dramatically in price in recent years, while their processing and storage capabilities have increased to the point where they are more powerful than mainframe systems of the late 1960s. Software packages have similarly fallen in price while having improved in quality, reliability and features offered. Given these advancements it is only the smallest business which cannot cost-effectively use a micro or larger computer system for operating its sales ledger. Ideally, the sales ledger software should be part of an integrated accounting system package since this could save considerable time in posting entries, and reconciling and preparing accounts.

Computerised sales ledgers are usually 'open-time' type ledgers which only show unpaid items on the account after it has been closed each month. The history of customer's purchases and payments can be accessed by interrogating the database, usually by using a reporting facility which is part of the software package.

Open-item ledgers show the outstanding items and current balance for a customer's account, whereas the historical-type ledger, usually manually prepared, shows all transactions on a customer account from the date it was opened.

Reporting

The control of debtors requires the use of information available from the sales ledger. The two most common control measures used are days sales outstanding (DSO) ratios, and aged debtors analysis reports. Other reports are also used.

1. Days sales outstanding, is sometimes referred to as the debtor turnover period, which is a measure of the average days sales

outstanding in the debtors ledger. The DSO should be low; if it is high then credit control is insufficient. It is usually calculated as:

$$DSO = \text{period end debtors} \times \frac{\text{days in period}}{\text{sales in period}}$$

The problems with using DSO as a measure of control arise from:

- Distortions due to fluctuating sales.
- Accounting periods which are inconsistent with credit terms or customer payment cycles.
- Outstanding balances unduly influenced by promotions or receipt of cash discounts.
- The mix of cash and credit sales varying over time.
- Settlement of large accounts just prior to the period end causing distortions.

One refinement on this measure is to substitute average for period-end trade debtors as to some extent this reduces the distortion caused by taking a balance at a point in time. A further refinement is to calculate the DSO for major groups or credit categories of customer, so highlighting a particular group of slow payers hidden within the total DSO.

The DSO statistic is particularly useful when compared with similar businesses, or for a comparison within the same business over a period of time.

Another useful ratio for use in control of debtors is the bad debt ratio, calculated as:

$$\frac{\text{Bad debts incurred}}{\text{Total turnover on credit}}$$

This ratio should be monitored to ensure that turnover is not being increased at the expense of profitability, shown by an increase in the ratio. This ratio also reflects the effectiveness of the credit-control function within a business.

2. Aged debtor analysis is a report showing an aged analysis of each customer's account. It is one of the most useful documents for credit-control purposes. These reports should not only be

produced at month end but also at appropriate intervals during the month. As can be seen in Table 1.1, a typical report will include the credit limit and risk category, as well as the credit terms, age and amount overdue.

Table 1.1 *Customer aged analysis report*

Customer	Risk class	Credit term	Total	Current	1 Month	2 Month	3 Months or more
			£	£	£	£	£
AAA Ltd	'A'	Net monthly	50,000	30,000	10,000	7,000	3,000
BBB Ltd	'B'	Net monthly	30,000	15,000	10,000	5,000	–
YYY Ltd	'C'	Net monthly	20,000	12,000	6,000	1,000	1,000
ZZZ Ltd	'D'	Net monthly	100,000	71,000	10,000	9,000	10,000
			200,000	128,000	36,000	22,000	14,000
Percentage of customers			100	64	18	11	7

Another report commonly used to review the level and age of debtors is the debtors control report, shown in Figure 1.1. This report combines information in terms of days, pounds and per cent, showing the amount outstanding for each invoice at the end of each month.
3. Exception reports. It is not possible for a business with a large customer base to review regularly the status of all its customers' accounts. In these cases credit-control information should be produced highlighting exceptions from a predetermined norm such as a budget, target or the agreed terms.

Where the sales ledger is computerised it is usual to have either a reporting package (as part of the software suite) or bespoke programmes which can access sales ledger data to produce various reports. Reports may be specified which list overdue accounts within the following parameters:

- All.
- High-risk class.
- Exceeded credit limit.
- Balance outstanding of more than £5,000.

Date: 30 Nov

£000s		Invoiced in:					Total	Days
		Nov	Oct	Sept	Aug	pre-Aug		
Outstanding at end of:	Aug				£18.6 100%	£15.1	£33.7	37
	Sept			£30.4 100%	£3.4 18%	£2.8	£36.6	40
	Oct		£21.8 100%	£7.4 24%	£0.7 4%	£0.2	£31.1	34
	Nov	£20.2 100%	£6.1 28%	£2.0 6%	£0.0 0%	£0.0	£28.3	31

Figure 1.1 *Debtors Control Report*

- Overdue by more than 60 days.
- Overdue by 30 days with a balance of more than £10,000 and in a high risk class.

Reports can be selected on any combination of data on the ledger.

In order to control debtors it is useful to use targets, budgets and forecasts as yardsticks against which to measure current levels. Management can use these to motivate the staff responsible for collection and to highlight areas out of control which need further managerial attention.

Credit-control information should be prepared at different levels of detail depending on the user of the information. Senior management may, for example, require information on the total company, highlighting seriously overdue accounts. Credit control and sales staff would require varying levels of detailed information right down to transactions posted to a particular account.

Collection of Amounts Due

Having set up an information system to monitor customer payment performance it is necessary to use this information to pursue overdue accounts. Good credit-control management requires the existence of a policy for dealing with such accounts. This policy should be formulated after consideration of the following five points:

1. Customer type – major accounts should be treated differently from small domestic accounts.
2. Customer risk – low-risk customers should not be pursued as avidly as high-risk customers.
3. Age of debt – when and how often to prompt or take further action.
4. Size of debt – it is unlikely to be financially justifiable to take legal action over debts of less than, say, £50.
5. Credit-control resources – is sufficient time and expertise available within the business, or is outside help required?

It is inevitable that any business with a large customer base will experience varying degrees of adherence to the agreed payment terms. Non or late payment may be due to a number of factors, including:

Inability. Where a customer is unable to settle his account this could be due to temporary circumstances. In such a case it may be advisable to agree to a series of repayments over a period of time. Where the difficulty appears to be serious and showing no signs of improving a writ should be immediately issued. No further goods should be supplied.

Inefficiency. Here the cause may be due to poor systems or procedures, or poor quality or badly managed personnel. System changes, particularly where computerisation is involved, can cause inefficiencies but these should at worst be temporary. It may be better in the short term to accept payment delays due to inefficiency, but it should be made clear to the customer that terms should be adhered to as soon as possible to prevent further action.

Dissatisfaction. It is common for customers to withhold payments of thousands of pounds because of dissatisfaction with the quality of one batch of goods costing say one hundred pounds. In such cases it is reasonable to seek payment, less a deduction, for the amount in dispute. Better still the cause of dissatisfaction should be eliminated as soon as possible by giving a credit note when faulty goods are returned or by promptly taking whatever action is necessary. Dissatisfaction should not be permitted as an excuse for nonpayment of undisputed items.

Policy. Some customers have a deliberate policy of delaying payment and are therefore partly financing their businesses through their suppliers. This policy may be blatant if the customer is in a strong marketing position or may be disguised through a number of excuses and delaying tactics. Either way it should not be allowed and either extended credit terms should be agreed, or action taken, to bring the account within agreed terms.

Prompting payment

There are six main ways in which an overdue debt can be pursued, involving the use of customer statements, letters, telephone calls, and/or visits. If these do not result in payment, it will be necessary to consider stopping the supply of goods and withdrawing credit.

Statements. These are often used as the first reminder, though it is debatable how effective they are in prompting payment. In some instances a customer will not pay until he has received and reconciled the supplier statement. In larger businesses, however, with pressures to reduce costs, many bought-ledger departments do not have time to look at statements and merely throw them in the bin.

When issued, statements should:

- Highlight text emphasising credit terms and noting overdue items.
- Use bold, coloured lettering.
- List the balance due at the end of the previous period and all invoices/cash payments during the month.
- Be sent out as soon as possible after the month end.

Letters. These are the usual follow-up document where the customer base is large. They can be framed in varying degrees of intensity from a polite reminder to a threat of legal action. In most instances two letters are sufficient. In some trades the only letter sent is that threatening suspension of supplies and legal action to recover the debt.

Effective follow-up letters should be:

- Brief, polite and lucid.
- Properly addressed, preferably naming the individual who can take action (normally the senior financial executive, in the case of the final reminder).
- Sent at the appropriate time. This depends on frequency of supplies, credit terms, and customer-payment systems.
- Sent first class. Recorded delivery may have a psychological impact when used with final reminders.
- Well designed, using bold lettering and coloured ink to distinguish this from other correspondence and to highlight the significance of the letter.

The telephone. This is perhaps the most effective method of follow up. It is also personal, convenient and considerably cheaper than a letter when all costs, particularly administrative, are taken into account. A telephone call to the appropriate person can elicit immediate payment, whereas a letter may never reach him.

Effective use of the telephone requires training and experience. The following points must be covered when making a call.

- Preparation – the ledger should be scrutinised to ascertain payment history and outstanding amounts. The customer file should be read to find out when previous calls were made, who the contacts are and what position they hold.

● Purpose – depending on the stage reached in the collection process the following questions could be asked: Why has payment not been made? When will the next cheque be sent and how much will it be for? Why do the statement and cheque amounts differ? Request a reconciliation of the difference. If the call is made before a payment is due, the date and amount of payment could be requested.

It is common for excuses to be given when querying non-payment by telephone. These tend to become standard and well-worn; experienced callers should formulate an effective response.

When calling it is important to be polite but firm at all times. This is especially so when closing the call at which time the caller should agree a course of action (this could be sending a statement, with a cheque being sent by return). Confirm this agreement with the other party.

Personal visits can be made by either the salesman or credit-control representative. However, this is a time-consuming way of solving the problem.

Many companies prefer not to involve salesmen in payment collection for reasons of control, and fear that by turning the salesman into a debt collector his selling relationships will suffer. On the other hand, in certain circumstances, the salesman may be ideally suited for receiving the debt if he regularly visits and knows the customer. Some businesses motivate salesmen to aid payment collection by giving commission on collections, not on sales.

Credit-control representatives visit customers for one of two reasons. Increasingly they are being used to visit large customers to resolve particular problems with the account and to build relationships with appropriate personnel (buyer, purchase-ledger supervisor, accountant and so on) with the aim of soliciting better payment. The other reason for a visit by representatives is to collect outstanding payments.

It is fairly common to call on large customers to collect a cheque at the end of the month. This is particularly so when the credit manager has a target of days sales outstanding which he is motivated to achieve. Many public companies take such measures at the financial year end so that statements portray a favourable position. One multinational goes as far as sending its credit-control manager round the country entertaining major customers with the aim of collecting a cheque over dinner!

Where other methods have failed to elicit payment from a customer a personal visit can be effective. In such cases the collector has to see (preferably having made an appointment) the person responsible for payment. Persistence and stubbornness will usually be rewarded with a cheque. This is particularly so when payment is demanded in front of staff or customers, embarrassing the company into payment.

The threat of supplies being stopped. This can be useful in prompting slow payers to produce a cheque. Yet the decision to stop supplies is not always clear cut. It can only be effective where further supplies are required by the customer. In cases where the customer has alternative sources of supply a decision has to be made as to whether the cost of overdue payment is worth the risk of losing a profitable account.

Once delivery has been suspended, the customer's buyer should be notified when he next places an order. In larger firms the buyer may not be aware of slow payment of an account and will be in a position to organise prompt settlement, particularly if the order is critical to a manufacturing process. The salesman who services the account must also be notified of such action to save the embarrassment of taking orders which will not be fulfilled.

The decision to withdraw credit. Obviously this depends upon the circumstances of each case. This action always applies where supplies are stopped and can be applied to tardy payers where constant reminders and warnings have failed. Credit facilities should not be automatically restored on payment, especially if facilities have previously been withdrawn.

Professional debt collection

At some point all internal means of collecting a debt will become exhausted and external collection means must be considered. These include the use of agencies and the instigation of legal proceedings.

A debt-collection agency. Agencies can do little more than a well-run credit-control department, and its involvement can upset customer relations while incurring a significant cost in the process. Agencies can, however, have a place in the collection cycle where:

- The customer base is large and the credit-control department has insufficient resources to deal with all overdue accounts. In such cases it is cost-effective to handle internally the large accounts and hand the smaller accounts over to an agency.
- The credit control staff are inexperienced or lack expertise.
- The agency has specialist knowledge of the trade.

There are many agencies in the UK providing debt-collection services. Most of these agencies also provide the credit-vetting services described earlier in this chapter. By far the most common type of agency is the commercial business. A number of trade associations also provide a collection service. These bodies are non-profit making and usually charge an enrolment fee and annual subscription, taking a percentage of debts recovered.

Some agencies charge a fee irrespective of whether the debt is recovered. This arrangement is becoming less common with most business being conducted on a 'no collection, no fee' basis. The usual collection process commences with a short, sharp letter followed by an intensive telephone follow-up until the account is settled.

A recently introduced method of collection, of American origin, is the voucher system. A business buys a book of collection vouchers and sends one back to the agencies with completed details of the debtor. The agency sends out a series of letters, each getting stiffer, over a period of weeks, with the aim of having the debt paid directly to the supplier. If this does not work, telephone calls or personal visits are made, either for a fixed fee or a percentage of cash collected. Larger agencies may even handle legal action through their solicitors.

With so many agencies to choose from, some being more reputable than others, the following points should be checked before deciding which one to use:

- Is it financially sound? Normal credit-vetting procedures should be followed.
- Are the directors and senior staff fully bonded?
- Is the agency licensed for debt collection under the Consumer Credit Act, 1974?
- Are clients' funds kept in an audited client trust account at its bank?
- Is the agency able to provide satisfactory references regarding its services?
- Are the fees competitive?

Having selected an agency, you must monitor its effectiveness. You might subsequently decide to dispense with its services or appoint another agency in the expectation that it will do a better job.

Instigating legal proceedings. This is the ultimate step in the collection cycle. It is costly both in terms of time and effort taken by a business' own personnel, and in solicitors' fees and court cost which may be incurred.

Legal action is usually taken where the debt is of sufficient size to more than offset the costs of the action, and where there is a reasonable likelihood of the debtor being able to pay. Some businesses have a policy of taking legal action irrespective of the size of debt to discourage other poor payers. The minimum amount over which it is worth taking legal action depends on particular circumstances, but it is unlikely that a debt of less than £50 could be recovered cost-effectively. If the amount owing is less than £5,000 the creditor can take legal action himself through a (normally his own local) County Court.

Claims for less than £500 are automatically dealt with by arbitration, unless the Registrar agrees to order a court trial. In such cases the proceedings are informal and the Registrar usually acts as the arbitrator. Solicitors' fees are not recoverable, although court costs, involving the summons and enforcement, can be regained. Fees paid to expert witnesses and travel costs, where incurred, are also recoverable. An excellent guide to the procedure for recovering debts in the County Court is contained in a free booklet, *Small Claims in the County Court,* issued by the Lord Chancellors' Department. Copies are obtainable, free of charge, from County Courts. Where the creditor does not wish to take action himself, or where the debt is over £5,000, a solicitor should handle the case.

The solicitor will normally start proceedings by writing to the debtor advising that legal proceedings will be commenced if the debt is not paid within seven days. If the debt is not paid by the specified date, and the creditor wishes to proceed, the solicitor will issue a writ through the High Court. Where the action is defended, costs are likely to escalate and the solicitor should advise the creditor as appropriate. If it is undefended, judgement will be obtained in the creditor's favour. However, if the money is still not repaid, you may have to issue an enforcement procedure.

A free publication, *Enforcing Money Judgements in the County Court,* issued by the Lord Chancellor's Department, advises on the methods of collecting money from the debtor. If a County Court judgement for £10 or more remains unsatisfied for more than 28 days, it is registered in the Unsatisfied County Court Judgement Register. This is open to public inspection and can adversely affect a debtor's credit status.

The most common method of enforcement is a Warrant of Execution. The court bailiff is ordered, by the court, to go to the debtor's premises and seize and sell suitable goods with a view to realising the amount owed. The seizure is preceded by a warning note advising of the intended action if the debt, costs and bailiff's fee are not paid. In the case of a High Court judgement a Writ of Execution is the equivalent instrument by which the debtor's goods may be seized and sold. In such cases it is the Sheriff of the County who takes the action.

Garnishee orders can also be a very effective method of enforcement. These are used where a third party owes the debtor money and includes the debtor's bank where appropriate. The creditor applies to the court, on affidavit, for the issue of a summons to be served on the third party. When the garnishee order is made absolute, the third party is ordered to pay the money over to the plaintiff.

Bankruptcy proceedings can be taken against individuals or partnerships owing more than £200. The Court hears the bankruptcy petition and, if satisfied, appoints an Official Receiver (usually a firm of Chartered Accountants) who seizes and sells any assets. The proceeds are distributed amongst creditors according to strict order or precedence commencing with secured creditors. Any residue is left to the bankrupt individual. The threat of such proceedings can be very effective, for an undischarged bankrupt is severely restricted in many ways.

An unsatisfied judgement against a limited company may be enforced through the filing of a winding-up petition. If the Court decides to issue a compulsory winding-up order, the company's assets are liquidated. Creditors are then paid according to legal order of precedence, commencing with secured creditors, which include all Government bodies who are always paid in full before any other creditors, both secured and unsecured, leaving any residue to be paid to preferential shareholders and finally unsecured creditors and ordinary shareholders.

Where a limited company owes more than £200, a statutory demand for payment can be made. In such cases, a Court judgement is not required and the creditor need only serve 21 days notice of his intention to file a petition for the compulsory winding-up of the company. This method is particularly effective in extracting payment from large companies whose ability to pay is not in question.

Purchasing protection against bad debts

Credit insurance and factoring are rather costly alternatives to a business bearing the cost of debts itself. However, there are circumstances under which they can be of use.

Credit insurance. This is where the failure of one or two major customers would have a serious impact on cash flow and profits. Most businesses insure their fixed assets, such as buildings, machinery and equipment against loss or damage. A significant proportion of overseas debtors are also usually insured. However, domestic debtors are not insured to anywhere near the same extent. The reason for this is that credit insurance is expensive and restrictive.

The advantage of credit insurance to a business is that it reduces or negates the effect of bad debts on profits and cashflow. It can be of particular benefit where a business trades significantly with one or two large customers. · In certain circumstances credit insurance may allow a business to increase sales. This occurs where the insured limit is above the business' normal credit ceiling.

A business must equate the cost of insurance against the risks involved and determine if the circumstances are such that insuring is justified. The alternative is to accept the risk and create a provision for bad debts, rather than pay insurance premiums.

Prior to granting a credit-insurance policy the insurer normally undertakes a review of the business credit-control procedures and insists on improvements where deemed necessary. Insurers often insist that the insured submits the whole of his customer list and not just the risky ones. Having submitted suggested limits for each customer the insurer decides whether to agree or reject particular customers and limits. Some policies may cover particular customers only, or all customers with an indebtedness above a certain limit.

The level of cover (indemnity) is normally between 75 and 90 per cent of the sale value, up to an agreed credit limit. Premiums vary according to the level of risk and on the insurer's normal terms, but are usually between 0.25 and 1 per cent of turnover.

Debt factoring. This is the sale of debts by a supplier to a third party (a 'factor') at a discount in return for cash. The services offered by a factor include:

- Making cash payments to the supplier in advance of the customer's debt payment. Cash advances of between 70 and 80 per cent of the invoice value are advanced to the supplier on receipt of invoices by the factor. The balance of the invoice value, less fees, is passed to the supplier either on receipt of cash from the customer ('pay as paid') or after a specified period ('maturity').
- Undertaking sales-ledger administration. Professional accounting and collection services are offered by most factors. The factor will keep the sales ledger, undertake the necessary credit control and collect the debts. The supplier is left only with the task of issuing invoices, normally using the factor's letterheading.
- Providing 100 per cent protection against bad debts.
- Providing credit advice on a customer's creditworthiness.

Generally, a factor will only act for a customer whose turnover is greater than £100,000, has an average invoice value of more than £100 and whose credit terms are less than 90 days. Factoring is usually only suitable for businesses where the credit risks arise primarily from the customer's credit-worthiness. It is not suitable for businesses selling to the public, or selling to one or two customers only, or involved in contracts incorporating stage payments.

The advantages that a factor can offer, particularly to a growing, small or medium-sized business include:

- A source of finance for expansion or acquisition.
- Saving of management time on collection and administration duties.
- Savings of the cost of credit control and sales ledger departments. These include savings on legal and administrative costs.
- Provision of regular management reports for use in decision

making and planning.

- Protection against bad debts, loss, and the consequent safeguard this has on profits.

The cost of a factoring service varies. When cash advances are made, and sales-ledger administration is provided, the costs are generally made up of a fee of 0.5 to 3 per cent of invoice value, with a further charge for interest on the amount advanced of between 2 and 4 per cent above bank base-lending rates.

Factoring can have drawbacks, such as the objections of customers to the introduction of a third party in its business relationships. At some point in a business' growth cycle it becomes more cost effective to establish internal sales-ledger and credit-control departments. Having relied on a factor for a number of years, it can be difficult to change.

The Credit Department

In small businesses the credit-management duties are commonly the responsibility of the accountant or owner. Eventually a business will grow to such a size that it is necessary to establish a credit department, with a manager who is responsible for ensuring cash inflow and minimising bad debts.

In the UK it is usual for the credit manager to report to the senior financial executive. Some argue he should report to the managing director to ensure independence. It is extremely unadvisable for him to report to the sales manager, as there is an obvious conflict of interest.

The credit manager is often responsible for the operation of the sales ledger. This is advisable because an up to date well run ledger is the prime source of credit-control information. Depending on the size of the business it will be necessary to have a number of clerks for sales-ledger and credit-control duties. There is no definitive way of organising these personnel. They may all carry out both sales-ledger and credit-control duties or specialise in one. Some organisations deploy clerks working in pairs, one covering credit control and the other the sales-ledger administration for a range or customers. When deciding on the organisation of the department it is important to recognise the different skills required for ledger and credit-control work. Credit-control clerks should have communication skills for use on the telephone, whereas these are not required for ledger work.

As with any good organisation the structure and reporting lines should be clearly defined. Duties should be clearly identified, preferably in the form of a detailed description which emphasises principal accountabilities.

Training of credit department staff should normally be one of the credit manager's principal duties. An excellent starting point for training is to have a procedures manual for the department. This should detail the business' credit policy and clearly document the key tasks and routines of each member of staff.

Regular 'on-the-job' training is the normal method of practical training. This can be supplemented by appropriate seminars, courses and directed private study as appropriate.

For those wishing to make credit control their career, membership of the Institute of Credit Management is advantageous and advisable. To become a member it is necessary to pass the Institute's examinations and gain relevant practical experience. Dun and Bradstreet run a correspondence course in credit and financial analysis which gives a useful theoretical foundation to those starting work in the credit department.

As with all areas of business, credit management must adapt to changes in business climate and legislation, and a host of other factors. To keep up to date it is necessary to ensure regular training is received by all credit-control staff, including the manager.

2
Cash Payment

The cash-payment cycle is, in many ways, a mirror image of the cash-collection cycle. As with the collection cycle it involves three important considerations: interest costs, administrative costs and supplier relationships. Businesses must contend with the same commercial and financial environment to achieve the minimum possible interest cost of working capital. Administrative systems must be effective in terms of controlling payment while incurring minimum operating costs. Both these costs are constrained by the fact that supplier relationships can be harmed if payments are not made in line with agreed terms.

The payment cycle which commences when an order is placed and finishes when value has been lost (when the business' bank account has been debited) can be shown diagramatically.

Figure 2.1

The elements of the payment cycle can be closely interrelated and, depending upon the business and its environment, may be combined. This is particularly true where cash is payable on order, or on receipt of goods.

Invoice Processing

Procedures. A business should have proper procedures for ensuring that purchase invoices are registered, checked, authorised and posted quickly and efficiently. Physical control procedures should also be in place to ensure that the goods received are of the correct type and quantity ordered, and of acceptable quality.

Orders. The invoice-processing system starts when an order has been placed. A copy of the order should be passed to the accounts payable department. When the goods are delivered they should be verified to ensure that they correspond to the delivery note and/or associated invoices. Damages or shortages should be notified to the accounts payable department. Many well-run businesses will raise a goods received note (GRN) and pass a copy to the accounts payable department for use in invoice processing.

Invoices. When the invoice is received it should be passed immediately to the accounts-payable department for registering. Invoices have often been lost without trace where a register is not used. This can lead to nonpayment and a deterioration of supplier relations. A further advantage of registering the details of an invoice (sequential number, supplier, date, amount and description of goods or service) is that the invoice register can be useful for calculating accruals at the accounting period end, and for determining short-term cash requirements.

Where standard components are concerned, the invoiced price, quantity and credit terms should be verified against the signed purchase order and goods received note. If all agree the invoice should be passed for payment. Many businesses set control limits for differences between purchase-order price and invoice price. If differences are within the preset tolerance the invoice will be passed for payment; if not, the invoice is usually referred to the buyer or purchase manager to resolve or approve the difference. In cases where there is no purchase order, (for example, where a service has been provided), the invoice should be passed to the appropriate manager with authority to sign the invoice as evidence of approval. It is good practice for the accounts-payable department to keep a register of such invoices as delays often occur due to the invoice finding its way to the bottom of a busy manager's in-tray.

Significant administrative costs are incurred in invoice processing, both in terms of the people involved and in the systems used. A business should regularly review its processing system to ensure tasks and paperwork are not duplicated. Appropriate procedures should be in place to ensure that management time is not taken up with routine queries which could be resolved by the accounts-payable clerks. In larger businesses computerisation can be used to advantage in the recording of orders placed and deliveries received, in batching invoices for posting to the ledger, and in generating a cheque and remittance advice.

Personnel costs may be reduced through careful organisation of staff, particularly in the accounts-payable department. By designating specific suppliers accounts to particular people, a natural focus for supplier queries concerning major accounts is formed. Such action can avoid duplication of effort and reduces uncertainty about what action has been taken. Suppliers generally prefer a particular contact with whom they can develop a relationship.

Speed and timing

Delays in passing an invoice for payment can adversely affect supplier relations if they lead to settlement delays. They can also lead to the loss of attractive discounts. Where the normal processing time is longer than the discount qualifying period, steps should be taken to identify such invoices and ensure the necessary steps are taken to expedite their processing. One particular business requires all invoices to be passed to the accounts-payable supervisor, who personally identifies invoices offering discounts. The supervisor processes these invoices, and personally ensures appropriate managerial approval is obtained where necessary.

The time taken from receipt of invoices to posting to the accounts-payable system should be regularly monitored to ensure that excessive delays are eliminated.

Invoice Payment

A business should ensure that procedures are in place to determine the maximum length of credit which can be obtained from each supplier and to ensure that these payment rules are followed unless special circumstances prevail.

Credit terms. Also called terms of payment, were discussed at some length in Chapter 1 on Cash Collection. It is obviously of benefit to a business to maximise length of credit taken. However, discounts must be considered. A business should take up discounts only where the discount is greater than the opportunity cost of early payment, and/or the costs of separately handling these earlier payments was small.

A business' policy towards the credit terms taken will involve deciding whether to supersede the supplier's credit terms with its own. This is now a practice commonly used by large companies. One multi-national company ignores supplier's terms and pays accounts at the end of the month following the month of invoice. This can mean that a supplier with terms stipulating 'net 30 days' has to wait up to 30 days longer than it expected before payment is received. Another policy decision often taken by large businesses involves processing payments on certain dates. If the supplier's invoices miss a processing run the customer may decide not to authorise a special payment and, where the processing cycle is monthly, a further monthly credit will be taken.

It can be useful for a business to compare the policy for the accounts-payable department with the timing of payments experienced by the credit-control department. Closer coordination may lead to new ideas on what is acceptable trade credit, and a business may also find that it can further delay the payment of some accounts.

Whilst creditors are a valuable source of finance, it should be appreciated that failure to pay invoices on time can damage relationships with suppliers and cause problems for the purchasing and production functions.

Evidence of deteriorating supplier relationships can manifest itself in several forms, notably:

- Less cooperation from suppliers.
- Increased prices.
- Deteriorating credit terms.
- Delayed deliveries.
- Supply stoppage.
- Legal costs.
- Difficulty in opening accounts with new suppliers (through having gained a poor reputation in the industry).

A business must weigh up the long-term implications of slow payment against the attractions of increasing short-term finance at the expense of its suppliers.

Procedures

As well as the agreed credit terms, the time taken by a business to pay its suppliers is determined by the systems and procedures in the business.

Controls. All internal processing controls should be completed before payment is made.

Availability of funds. Payment cannot be made if the business does not, at the due time, have funds available.

Management policy. Where payment is delayed beyond the due date, it should be a deliberate business policy, not the decision of an accounts payable clerk. A business should ensure that its policy regarding credit term is fully understood by all accounts payable and purchasing personnel. Just as accounts payable clerks should not take decisions to delay payments to suppliers, they should not pay before the due date.

Processing systems

The timing of payments is also governed to an extent by the processing systems which a business uses. Many businesses use computer facilities with batch-payment systems which significantly reduce administration cost. With such systems there is normally one, monthly, payment run. Exceptions, such as invoices offering settlements discounts and seriously overdue accounts, can be dealt with manually at appropriate intervals during the month. As well as their cost-effectiveness, such systems are beneficial in aiding better cashflow forecasting. The number of payments made outside the normal payment run should be monitored from time to time to see whether more frequent processing of smaller batches would be more cost effective.

Reaction of suppliers

Some businesses take advantage of suppliers who do not pursue overdue debts. They do this by extending the payment cycle so as to retain both the goods and the cash in their own business for as long as possible.

One major company divided its suppliers into one of four categories:

- 'A' – offering discounts.
- 'B' – providers of strategic materials or having aggressive and prompt follow-up procedures if payment is delayed.
- 'C' – reacting to delayed payment after two weeks.
- 'D' – reacting very slowly to late payment.

The company had a fully-computerised, batch-processing

system which generated a remittance advice and cheque on a monthly cycle. Each month the chief accountant, senior buyer and accounts-payable supervisor scrutinised the payments to decide when to post the cheques to suppliers. Category 'A' cheques were sent out in time to take advantage of the discount and a few days grace! 'B' cheques were sent out within agreed terms. 'C' cheques were delayed one month and 'D' cheques sent out later and later each month until their suppliers resistance points were found. Suppliers were moved between categories depending on the degree of follow up experienced by the supervisor and senior buyer.

Methods of payment

The methods of making payment include cash, cheques, bank transfers, bankers drafts and direct debits, each of which has been discussed in the context of the collection cycle (Chapter 1). When a business decides which method to use in paying suppliers it should consider the trade-off that exists between saving interest by late payment, and the need to maintain good supplier relations.

Businesses prefer to retain control over final payment of supplier accounts to gain flexibility in managing their liquidity and in dealing with disputes on goods or services received. It is for these reasons that cheques are the most commonly used methods as payment cannot be made unless initiated by the buyer. The supplier initiates the payment where direct debits or drafts are used, and it is normal for the supplier to have offered some inducement to gain the buyer's acceptance.

Significant administrative costs can be incurred where cheques or transfers are used to settle suppliers' accounts. They involve either clerical time or computer systems in their preparation, and managerial time in signing. Automatic signing machines can reduce such cost but are only appropriate where a high volume of low-value cheques is involved. Direct debits for a buyer involve the lowest administrative costs.

A business must decide to what extent it is prepared to compromise control and administrative costs. In the UK the most common method of payment is the cheque with bank transfer, through the Bankers Automated Clearing System (BACS). International payments are commonly made through mail or telegraphic transfers with bills of exchange also being used.

Payment of Other Creditors

Delayed payment of salaries and taxes, such as Value Added Tax (VAT), Corporation Tax and National Insurance, are similar to trade credit in that they are a spontaneous source of a business' financing. But they differ from trade credit in that a business is relatively constrained in terms of what it can do to influence these items as a source of financing.

All employees of a business are a source of finance since they are not paid for their services as these are provided. Instead, they are normally paid at the end of the week or the month. For businesses engaged in a seasonal trade, wages and salaries represent a spontaneous and flexible source of financing. During the busier part of the year when more employees are engaged in a production process, the amount of financing available from wages and salaries increases. A business' management can do little to influence this source of financing. Some leeway does exist because the business could choose to pay its employees less frequently, say, monthly instead of weekly. Similarly, payment by cheque rather than cash will provide a few extra days credit.

The government can be the source of considerable short-term finance to a business. Corporation Tax due on profits earned is not due for payment until some time after the profits have been earned. Although interest is charged on overdue payments it has been known for some businesses to delay tax payments because the interest penalty was lower than the cost of borrowings that could be obtained elsewhere! National Insurance and Pay As You Earn (PAYE) deductions are due on a specified date each month, but this is some time after deducting the payments from employees. Little can be done to increase the funding available from this source. VAT payments are usually due quarterly and any delay in remitting due payment is now met with draconion penalties. A business failing to pay VAT on the due date is liable to fines up to 30 per cent of the payment due.

Payments to employees and government represent a significant part of a business' total cash flow. Relationships with employees and ultimately with government departments are no less important than supplier relationships. Great care should therefore be taken to weigh up the benefits of delaying payment and improving/retaining good employee/government department relationships.

Reporting on Creditors

The management of creditors is important because tight control over payments made to them provides an easy and cheap way of obtaining finance. For this policy to be effective, a responsive reporting system is essential.

Financial reports should be used to monitor balances owed to creditors. These reports should be produced promptly and frequently with summary figures sent out to the appropriate levels of senior management. The reports should contain the following financial indicators.

- Credit payment period*
- Age analysis of creditors
- Total value of creditors
- Actual *vs* budget performance
- Actual *vs* forecast performance
- Actual *vs* past performance
- Actual *vs* performance of comparable businesses.

Note:
The credit payment period is calculated as:

Average or period end trade creditors
Average daily purchases in the period

Internal Controls

Fraud and error are always potential dangers within a creditor's system, so a business should take steps to introduce the appropriate degree of internal controls. Preventative checks and monitoring controls are necessary in order to ensure that:

- Payment is only made in respect of goods and/or services supplied.
- Payment is made to the right creditors.
- Payment is only made once.
- Appropriate discounts are taken at the correct time.

The level of internal control applied within a business will depend upon its size and circumstances. The following preventive measures are recommended to ensure good control.

- There should be a separation of functions within the business. Different personnel should be responsible for verifying the receipt of goods, for recording the liability to pay, and for authorising and making the payment.
- There should be a clear division of tasks within the accounts-payable department. Where possible, different personnel should be allocated the tasks of preparing and checking documents from those recording the details in the books of account (writing up the invoice register, entering invoice details on the purchase ledger). Strict controls should be in force for the opening of new creditor accounts and authorisation should normally be required from a senior financial manager.
- Purchase orders should be made in writing and be signed by an authorised employee.
- Invoices should only be authorised for payment when all documents (GRN, purchase order and invoice) have been cross checked and signed by an authorised signatory when appropriate.
- Invoices should be stamped 'Paid' when the instruction is given, to prevent them from being paid twice.

- Supplier statements should be reconciled to verify outstanding balances and as a check on the efficiency of the payment system.
- Debit balances on creditors' accounts should be investigated as this could indicate a prepayment or, more seriously, a wrong payment.

It is useful for a business to carry out an occasional internal audit of all its procedures. Such a review should cover all aspects of the goods-movement system within the business with a view to improving efficiency as well as reducing the likelihood of fraud or error.

3
Stocks

Stock, often referred to as inventory, can be defined as any current asset held for conversion into cash in the normal course of trading. It can be classified into one of three distinctive types:

1. Raw materials. These represent purchased items awaiting conversion into saleable products and are usually found in manufacturing businesses.
2. Work-in-progress. This consists of materials, components or products in various stages of completion during a manufacturing process. The term also applies to partly completed contracts or partially provided services.
3. Finished goods. These are manufactured goods, ready for sale or dispatch to a customer.

In most industries, stocks of finished goods must be held in order to satisfy the needs of customers. The resulting investment in stocks often makes heavy demands on working capital, particularly when a business is growing or when inflation is high. In the manufacturing industry, raw material and work-in-progress stocks increase these demands. Given that stocks in manufacturing businesses can often account for half the total assets employed, careful planning and control of stocks can significantly improve profitability and liquidity.

Stock Policy

Stock policy is derived through the 'trade-off' between the cost and benefits of holding stock. Shortages of stock can be costly in terms of lost orders, lost production and idle time. However, maintaining excessive stock results in additional holding costs and increases the amount of working capital required. A business should consider each of these factors when deciding on an optimum stock-holding policy.

Need for stocks

If production and delivery of goods were instantaneous, there would be no need to hold stock except as a hedge against price increases. Despite rapid advances in computerisation and automation the goods-movement process still does not function quickly enough to avoid the need for holding at least some stocks. Finished goods stock must be held so that the customer can be serviced immediately, or at least quickly enough to ensure that he does not turn to another supplier. In turn, production operations cannot flow smoothly without having stocks of raw materials and work in progress.

Stocks are cushions to absorb planning errors and fluctuations in supply and demand. They also facilitate smooth production and marketing activities. Furthermore, they help minimise the interdependence of all parts of a business; for example, the production department could continue to produce in anticipation of future orders through the build up of finished goods stock.

Stock costs

The cost of stock consists of three elements; its purchase price, the holding costs and the cost to the business of being out of stock. The purchase price is an obvious cost, but the other costs are often less so.

Holding costs

The cost of holding stock varies widely from business to business and from industry to industry. As a crude rule of thumb the cost of holding stock for one year is in the region of 25p for every £1 of stock held. Holding costs include purchasing, storage and warehousing, handling, insurance, the cost of working capital, stock control and administration, and stock obsolescence.

Purchasing. One of the principal holding costs is that of procurement. These costs relate to finding suitable suppliers, negotiating terms and placing orders. The costs are made up of staff salaries and wages, National Insurance, pensions, office accommodation, equipment and overheads such as telephone, telex, stationery, light and heat.

Storage and warehousing. Stocks occupy space which is an expensive and scarce resource. The more obvious costs associated with storage space include rent, rates, light, heat, fire prevention, security, cleaning and maintenance. Other significant costs include the cost of employing stores and warehouse personnel, and storage equipment such as bins and racks.

Handling. Some businesses, particularly those in the heavy-engineering industry, have to invest significant amounts in equipment used for handling stocks. Heavy lifting gear, such as cranes, may be needed and the commonly used forklift trucks can be very expensive.

Insurance. Insurance premiums are paid to cover the risks involved in stockholding. The risks relate not only to the stock itself, through loss due to fire, flood, pilferage, and so on, but also to buildings and equipment, and to the personnel involved (employers liability and public liability).

Cost of working capital. This is usually the largest cost associated with holding stock. When a business holds stock it incurs an interest cost. This may be the real cost of borrowed funds used to finance the stock or it may be the cost of other investment opportunities which could not be undertaken (the opportunity cost).

Stock control and administration. Costs associated with stock control and administration involve material requirements planning, monitoring and review. The cost elements involved are data processing costs such as computer software, hardware and running costs, and personnel costs. Personnel costs are incurred in many functions including management, materials requirement planning, internal audit and accounting.

Stock obsolescence. In many businesses, particularly in retail clothing where fashions constantly change, stock obsolescence can be a significant cost. Obsolescence costs relate to the diminished value of stock due to lower demand and therefore lower market price. The longer stock is held the greater is this stockholding cost likely to be.

Cost of being out of stock

The true cost of being out of stock is difficult to calculate accurately, but it is an important factor to consider when determining stock policy.

If a business runs out of finished goods stock it could lose a sale. In this case the 'cost' is the gross margin on orders lost as a direct result of being out of stock. There is also an indirect cost in that customer goodwill may be lost resulting in future orders going to competitors.

Shortages of raw material and work-in-progress stocks can lead to the shutdown of production operations. The costs here are those of idle labour and machines, and also the gross margin on the lost production (assuming all production can be sold). Further costs may be incurred if partially finished goods have to be reworked or if the shortage necessitates smaller, uneconomic production runs. Overtime working is often necessary to meet back orders and the premium involved is a further cost of being out of stock. Other 'stock-out' costs include buying in alternative materials or buying from alternative, more expensive suppliers.

If a business is contracted to supply a product by a certain date stock shortages may lead the customer to invoke penalty clauses if delivery is late. Such costs can be considerable.

Stock Control Techniques

Good stock control aims to ensure that the optimum stock level is established and maintained. This involves deciding on the optimum stock level for each item, the timing and amount of stock to re-order, and ascertaining the permitted frequency of stock-outs.

Stock control classifications

An effective stock-control system will not have all items in stock treated in the same way or be liable to the same control techniques. Some businesses control part of their stock by the 'two-bin' system. Normally applied to low-value, highly used items this system does not rely on the maintenance of perpetual inventory records as is normal. Instead two bins are kept, and after the first bin is emptied, a withdrawal from the second bin triggers a re-order. A variation of this method is to re-order when a line appears on the bin having physically removed some stock.

Many businesses find it useful to divide raw materials and finished goods into subclassifications for stock-control purposes. The service division of a large electronics manufacturer, for example, carries over 50,000 spare parts in stock. The control system employed in this company is the widely used A-B-C method (otherwise known as 'distribution by value', 'Pareto principle' or '80–20 rule'). Here the stock items are ranked in order of decreasing usage value per item. If the ranking or distribution were plotted it would look similar to the figure below.

The stock distribution curve reveals a typical pattern; a small percentage of the items in stock constitues a large proportion of the total investment made by the business.

The degree of control required varies for each class of item. 'A' items require tight control because they represent a large percentage of total investment, and their high usage and value gives rise to the possibility of recording errors and pilferage. 'B' items will require lesser controls while 'C' items may only need slight attention. It is common to keep records (either stock cards

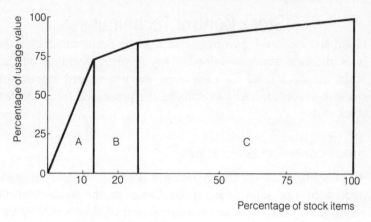

Figure 3.1 Percentage of usage value

or computer records) for 'A' and 'B' items, while 'C' items may be controlled by visual surveillance only.

The categorising of stock items in this way illustrates the principle of control. In practice businesses may have many more classifications, each of which is subjected to varying degrees of control.

Stock control models

Stock control requires policy decisions on the quantity of stock to be ordered and on the timing of those orders.

The quantity of stock to be ordered can be calculated by equating the costs of holding stock with the cost of acquiring the stock. Assuming a set demand for the goods, the cost of holding stock will be comparatively high with high-order levels; comparatively low with low order levels. Furthermore, the cost of acquiring stock will be comparatively low with high order levels, as the business will not have to place orders so often, and comparatively high with low order levels. As one rises, the other falls, though not usually at the same rate. The aim is to arrive at an order level where the two are equal, or nearly equal, as the total cost of the order (of both holding and acquiring) will be lowest. This optimum size is called the economic order quantity (EOQ) and is normally calculated by a formula:

Economic order quantity =

$$\sqrt{\dfrac{2 \times \text{annual demand} \times \text{acquisition cost}}{\text{holding cost}}}$$

The basic formula is based on a number of assumptions. In addition, stock holding and acquisition costs may not be known accurately; but in most businesses good estimates are obtainable. This analytical approach to order quantity determination is useful in providing an indication of the economic order quantity, even though it may not be exactly due to the various assumptions and estimates made. It should be noted that as one of the largest holding-cost elements is the cost of working capital, as interest costs rise so the EOQ drops, often to the lowest order level possible.

The formula can be modified to take into account the lowest unit purchase price available on bulk purchases, as well as the minimum order values often imposed by suppliers.

The amount of stock to be ordered can be calculated using the economic order model. The question of when to order is dependent upon the lead time, which is the time interval between placing an order and receiving delivery, and stock usage during lead time. Lead time multiplied by the daily usage gives the minimum level of stock which should be held, and is commonly called the order point.

In reality businesses do not accurately know demand, and delays occur between the time deliveries are due and received. It is for these reasons that most businesses provide some safety stock. The order point is therefore commonly calculated as the safety stock plus the usage during the lead time.

The calculation of safety stock hinges on demand forecasts. Based on past experience it is possible to derive a probability distribution showing the chance of varying levels of daily demand. This distribution can be used for constructing the associated costs of maintaining safety stocks. The two main costs are stock holding and stock-out costs. The optimum safety-stock level exists where the costs of carrying an extra unit are exactly counterbalanced by the expected costs of being out of stock.

Under the 'A', 'B', 'C' stock classification, different levels of protection (safety stock) may be specified for different classes, depending on objectives. Some firms may specify 99 per cent in-stock condition for the fast-moving 'A' items, 90 per cent for 'B' items, and 80 per cent for 'C' items. Other companies might set the lowest safety-stock levels, along with the highest frequency of re-orders, for the high-cost class 'A' items and spend less re-ordering effort, at the cost of proportionately higher safety stocks, for the lowest cost class 'C' items.

The previously discussed stock control models revolved around the constant order quantity or fixed-order level system, that is, where stock levels reach a level of 'X' we order 'Y'. The other widely used model is the constant re-order cycle or fixed-interval system. Here the order date is fixed. The quantity ordered depends on the usage from the previous order and also the outlook during the lead time. Demand forecasts and seasonal patterns are also considered in specifying the size of orders during the year.

The minimisation of cost of stock is the prime objective, regardless of the system used. A constant-order *cycle* system has advantages over the constant-order *quantity* system where (a) the cost of continuous surveillance is too high, and/or (b) transportation and ordering economies can be gained through regular ordering of several different items from the same supplier. The major disadvantage of the constant-order cycle system is that it may require higher safety stocks.

Just-in-time manufacturing

Recently, there has been much interest in the concept of just-in-time (JIT) manufacturing, which originated in Japan. Many Japanese factories have a philosophy that stock of any kind is a bad thing not only because of stockholding costs, but also because stockholding is a way of covering up inefficiency of procurement, production and marketing.

JIT techniques aim to cut stocks to the minimum through

creating close relationships with suppliers. By working with a small number of suppliers, preferably close to the manufacturing plant, and placing long-term contracts, lead times can be reduced by having regular, reliable deliveries.

Errors in production planning, or a lack of flexibility in the procurement and production planning process, lead to high stocks. JIT addresses this problem through the use of a closed-loop manufacturing requirements planning (known as MRPII) system. Such a system leads to more accurate time-phased planning of materials and production.

Large batch sizes for the production of sub-assemblies and finished products lead to higher stocks. JIT addresses this problem by using techniques which reduce set-up times. Where large amounts of stock are held in queues on the shop floor awaiting the next stage in production, JIT techniques reduce WIP stock through improved factory layout.

A full discussion of JIT techniques and MRP systems is inappropriate in this book. However, the reader should be aware of their existence as they can significantly reduce stock levels in manufacturing industry.

Stock Recording and Reporting Systems

Stock recording and reporting systems are necessary to enable a business to manage the amount of working capital tied up in stock.

Stock records

Accurate stock records are the basis of any stock control system, and users of stock information must be able to rely on its accuracy if it is to be used for decision making.

Each individual item of stock has to be identified, coded and stored on a database. Codings may be numerical, alpha-numerical, bar coded or picture coded. When the coding system is being designed care must be taken to incorporate possible future requirements (the business may expand rapidly or diversify). Where large amounts of data are held, computerisation become necessary and coding must be carefully designed to accommodate this.

Stock movements must be recorded within the stock control system. Basic information on usage, replenishments, date, location, value and authorisation must be recorded whether the system used is manual or computerised. Sophisticated, real-time systems are now used in supermarket stores where items passing over a sensor on the checkout are recorded on the till and down dated on the stock record to show the current on-hand quantity. Such systems also generate purchase orders and provide historical turnover information and project forecast demand.

The use of the stock control models already discussed can be greatly facilitated if they are available on computerised systems. Various software packages exist which provide stock control facilities, varying from simple automated goods movement to sophisticated control systems such as the MRP packages, MAAPICS and COPICS. By using computers great improvements in control are possible which can be used to:

- Calculate batch sizes using a suitable model.
- Print out items on which stock-outs have occurred.
- Decide what items should be reordered.
- Print out purchase orders.
- Record and report the level of service being achieved by the stock control system.

As microcomputers are becoming more and more powerful and software packages more reliable and cost-effective, it is only the very small businesses which would not benefit from their use.

Stock counts

The usefulness of a stock control system relies heavily on the accuracy of the stock records which are used as a basis for decision making. Often the computerised database or stock-record card can show a large positive stock balance which cannot be physically located.

The ultimate control on stock records is achieved by counting the stock. This may be done by perpetual or cycle counting of various stock items at different times. Alternatively, all the stock may be counted at one go. Many businesses only count stock once a year as part of the requirements of preparing statutory accounts, and they make the appropriate adjustment to stock records at this time. For management-control purposes, particularly where many items of stock are concerned, this can be totally inadequate so more frequent counts should be organised.

Classification of stocks

The database for a stock control system consists of records, or individual items of stock detailing the nature, cost, location and stage of completion. Where numerous items are involved a good management-information system involves stock being classified into certain aggregate types. Such aggregations allow reduced administration costs and improve the decision-making process. Deciding on the degrees of aggregation depends upon the particular business' needs. In all cases, however, a balance must be struck between too many and too few classifications.

As we have seen, the most common classification is to group stocks by purpose, that is, raw materials, work-in-progress and finished goods. This classification enables management information to be directed to the user. The production function requires information on raw materials and work-in-progress, whereas the marketing function requires information on finished goods.

Within these categories a further breakdown is required. The production function normally requires information on materials for which there are no substitutes or which prevent an item continuing through the production process. The purchasing and production functions will require information on stock levels of items with a long lead time, such as supplies from overseas, as these can affect future production plans. Work-in-progress is often classified by the stage of production or by its physical location in the factory (often the two are the same). Many manufacturers have work-in-progress stages in departments reflecting the materials' flow through the factory.

Finished goods stock can be classified by major types, by market outlet (wholesale, retail and mail order) or by geographical area (home or export, northern or southern region, or town or city location of outlets). Stocks can be further classified within these groups, or can be separately classified by level of sales, age, security class (attractive items may need special control) or vulnerability to obsolescence or deterioration (fashionable clothes and fresh foods are relevant examples).

Management information

In order to control stock levels, reliable and timely information must be provided from the stock-recording system and be used by appropriate managers.

Management information on raw materials and work-in-progress stock is required by the production function so that production flows can be optimised. The production manager may, for example, require information on various raw materials so, if a particular component is in danger of being out of stock, he can re-schedule his production plan to produce an alternative product. Production managers need information on work-in-progress to ascertain the varying stages of completion of products. Such information may lead to a re-scheduling of workloads, require overtime work to clear bottlenecks or require a change in machine usage.

Information on finished goods stocks is required by the marketing function so that the ability to meet customer requirements can be ascertained. Such information may lead to revisions in marketing plans, such as altering advertising and promotional campaigns to accommodate the movement of fast or slow-moving items. Stock shortages may lead to the business buying in items from a competitor in order to provide a complete product range for customers.

Forecasts

As part of a business' management-information system it is necessary to prepare forecasts which are used in the stock-control system. Since stocks are held to supply customers' future needs some forecast of this demand is required. A business requires estimates of future sales demand, broken down into periods, particularly where sales are seasonal. Forecasts should be subjected to sensitivity analysis to indicate outcomes and risks under varying conditions.

From the sales forecast the effect on stock levels can be estimated and new stock-holding policies introduced if necessary. The forecasts may indicate a need to rebalance the type-mix in stock, change and location of stock, or raise or lower the level of stock. The sales forecast will have an effect on production plans as it may be necessary to increase production to build up stocks for a seasonal sales peak, or to curtail production of certain items to rebalance the stock profile.

Sales forecasts can be either subjective, based on a 'feel' for the market, or objective, taking account of current order size, historical sales and market trends. Statistical techniques, such as regression analysis, may be used when forecasting, or a computerised model created to simulate sales' patterns with varying parameters, showing price changes, advertising and promotional spend variations. Whatever method is used some forecast of future sales is necessary for stock control.

Ratio analysis

One of the most useful types of information for use in stock control is that of ratios. Ratios are easily understood by management and indicate the extent of stock control achieved. As with all ratios, one particular stock control ratio is of no great value in itself. Ratios should be compared over time, with any unexpected movement in the trend being investigated. Furthermore, ratios are more useful when compared against a budget, target or forecast; comparisons with similar businesses can be particularly useful indicators of relative efficiency.

The most commonly used ratio for indicating efficiency of

stock control is the stock turnover ratio:

Number of times stock turned over =
$$\frac{\text{Cost of sales for the year}}{\text{Average value of stock}}$$

In most cases the greater the number of times the stock is turned over per annum, the more efficient the stock control. A period of a year is normally taken for this ratio, but a shorter period is more appropriate for certain businesses, particularly in food retailing where stock can be moved quickly.

Instead of expressing stock in terms of turnover, it can be expressed in terms of time as follows:

Number of days of stock =
$$\frac{\text{Value of stock}}{\text{Average daily cost of sales}}$$

This ratio can give a warning of slow moving stocks as well as how many days stock should be kept on hand.

When the above ratios are calculated the cost of sales figure, not the sales figure, should be used, as consistent comparison requires actual sales to be on the same valuation basis as stocks, that is, cost not selling price.

Ratios should be computed for each class of stock, for example, raw materials, work-in-progress and finished goods. Within these classifications it is important to monitor particular items and sub-classifications of stock. Ratios for each of these should be calculated as is appropriate to the particular business.

Numerous other ratios may be calculated which may be appropriate to a particular business type. A few of the more common ratios are given below.

Slow-moving items ratio =
$$\frac{\text{Value of stock with a low turnover}}{\text{Total value of stock}}$$

Service level $=$
$$\frac{\text{Value of items supplied from stock}}{\text{Total cost of sales}}$$

Stores cost efficiency $=$
$$\frac{\text{Stores operating costs}}{\text{Stores issues out of stock}}$$

Stock reports

As with any management information, stock reports should have certain characteristics:

- *Timeliness* They should be produced at appropriate intervals, bearing in mind the costs involved in their preparation. Generally, the quicker information reaches management the more use it will have for decision-making purposes.
- *Accuracy Reports* should be as accurate as possible because sound decision-making must have a good factual basis.
- *Presentation* Good reports should be pleasing on the eye and easily readable.
- *Content* The content should be appropriate to the user, both in terms of the type of information contained in the report and in the level of detail displayed.

A business' stock reports should be designed to show information which is useful for that particular business. Also, they should be reviewed regularly to ensure that they continue to meet the users' needs in a changing environment. A typical stock report should contain some, or all of the following information.

- Stock turnover ratio.
- Number of days of stock.
- Absolute value.
- Percentage of slow moving items.
- Customer service level.
- Actual *vs* budget performance.

- Actual *vs* forecast performance.
- Actual *vs* last year's performance.
- Number of stock items.
- Number of out of stock items

The important point about stock information is that it should be of use to the recipient. The stock controller will require detailed information for supplying production requirements, whereas the financial director may require total information to monitor working-capital requirements.

Accounting for Stock

Stock accounting has two elements: a physical recording system that can record accurately and promptly all stock receipts, issues and balances; and a method of stock valuation that is consistent and appropriate to the type of business being undertaken. Since the first element has been covered earlier in this chapter we will now turn to stock valuation.

At some time a business must make a policy decision regarding the method of valuing stocks. This decision is important as it will directly affect the computation of the business profits. The chosen valuation method will be subject to judgements of acceptability by tax authorities and auditors for differing reasons. For financial reporting purposes the business must ensure that stocks are valued at the lower of cost or net realisable value.

In modern trading conditions the same items of material will be acquired at different prices depending upon the time they were bought. Three inventory valuation methods are commonly used, each of which will give rise to differing costs of the stocks used in any one period. Each, when matched with the sales in that period, will give rise to differing profits. The profits calculated differ only in terms of timing, not in the total amount generated. The three valuation methods are as follows.

1. First-in, first-out (FIFO). The earliest acquired stock is

assumed to be used first; the latest acquired stock is assumed to be still in stock.

2. Last-in, first-out (LIFO). The earliest acquired stock is assumed to be still in stock; the latest acquired stock is assumed to have been used immediately. The LIFO method applies the most recent stock costs as the cost of goods sold. It attempts to match the current cost of obtaining stock against sales for a period. As compared to FIFO, the use of LIFO will tend to result in lower profitability during periods of rising prices.

3. Weighted average cost. This is often used with a periodic inventory system and is calculated by dividing the total cost of the opening stock, plus purchases, by the total number of units in those two classes. Other methods of computing average inventory costs, for example, the moving average method, can also be used.

Whichever stock valuation method is used in a business it should be applied consistently over time to enable true performance comparisons to be made.

4
Managing Cash

The amount of internally generated cash available to a business depends on its trading performance, balance-sheet control, capital expenditure and dividend policy. Cash management involves maintaining internal controls over cash transactions and cash handling, preparing cashflow forecasts and monitoring cash balances with a view to maintaining the optimum position through funding and investment strategies.

Cash held by a business can include cash, cheques received, cheques paid but not sent, and money held in bank accounts, as well as promissory notes and bills of exchange. Special attention to the internal control of cash must be paid. Cash appeals to the human acquisitive instinct; a relatively small volume represents a considerable value, and it is one of the most easily convertible and untraceable assets.

Internal Controls

Proper internal control procedures should minimise losses due to errors, theft or fraud. Internal controls which should be maintained are as follows.

Separation of duties. A key element in any internal control system is the separation of duties or functions. This imposes checks on each individual, and increases the need for collusion between individuals before cash can be mis-appropriated. The following functions should be undertaken by different individuals:

- *Management* The authorisation of instructions to pay

(suppliers's invoice, employee expense claims or cash advance requisitions).

- *Recording* The recording in account books of cash expenditure and receipt. Where possible, each type of book should be maintained by a separate individual.
- *Custody* The receipt or payment of cash, and signing for that receipt or payment.
- *Control Receipts* and payments should be authorised and recorded through the use of vouchers.

This may be difficult in small businesses, in which case it is then necessary to increase supervision of those individuals carrying out the above functions.

Cash budgets. A cash budget should be prepared, providing an indication of the expected levels of cash and bank balances during the year. Actual balances should be compared with the budget, with differences being analysed and explained.

Physical safeguards. Blank cheques and cash balances should be made inaccessible to unauthorised personnel by means of physical barriers such as counters, cash-boxes and safes. Keys should be held by a responsible officer and made accessible only to authorised personnel. Ideally, safes should have two locks, the two keys being with different people. Conveyancing of cash should use special vehicles (armoured cars) with accompanying guards.

Procedures manual. The cashier should work to a procedures manual. The procedure should detail all aspects of the cashier's work including the method of custody and control over cash. The procedure should include a list of personnel who are authorised to sign payment orders. It should also contain specimen signatures along with types of payment and limits up to which they are allowed to sign. The procedure and timing of cash counts should be detailed.

Authorised signatures. Banks should be notified of authorised personnel and their signing powers, and they should be instructed to make payments only on written orders bearing the required signatures. Cheques of high value, say, over £100, should require two signatures.

Other desirable control measures include limitation on the number of bank accounts, the setting of a maximum amount for cash (as opposed to cheque) payments, and the setting of a maximum limit for cash holdings. This may require special trips to pay excess cash into a bank account.

Imprest system

Petty cash and other similar funds should be kept on an imprest system. It involves the cashier being advanced a cash float for a fixed amount. This is replenished regularly by the total payments made, less any receipts. The cash-in-hand plus the paid expense vouchers due for reimbursement, less receipts, should always be equal to the amount of the float. When the float is replenished the petty-cash book and the paid-expense vouchers should be produced to the signatories of the reim-bursement cheque for initialling and approval.

The imprest system is a simple and effective control over petty cash and similar funds, because it provides an automatic and regular review of the nature and level of cash expenditure when the reimbursement cheque is signed. It also prevents the cashier increasing the cash balance without the signatories' knowledge.

Bank reconciliation

The bank reconciliation is the prime control on a business cash balance and bank accounts. The control objectives of preparing a bank reconciliation are to verify the cash book against the bank's records to ensure that:

- No payments have been passed through the bank account which are not recorded in the cash book.
- No undue delay has occurred in paying receipts into the bank.

- No contra items, such as dishonoured cheques, which may have been paid into the bank to conceal a misappropriation, appear in the bank statement without being recorded in the cash book.

Bank balances, according to the cash book, should be reconciled regularly, at least monthly, with the balances shown by bank statements. The reconciliation should be prepared or, at least checked by, persons other than those involved in the payments or receipts function. Arrangements should be made for bank statements (and paid cheques) to be sent directly from the bank to the independent persons responsible for preparing the reconciliations. The reconciliation should include the following.

- A comparison of each debit and credit shown in the bank statement with the cash book.
- A comparison of the paid cheques (if available) with the cash book as to names, dates and amounts.
- A comparison of the detailed paying-in slips with the cash book.
- Inquiry into any contra items, either in the cash book or on the bank statements.
- A check that all outstanding cheques and receipts, recorded in the previous month's reconciliation, have passed through the bank account since the date of the reconciliation or appear on the current month's reconciliation. An independent check on the bank reconciliation should be carried out at regular intervals.

Controlling Cash Receipts

Internal control measures over debt collections should ensure that all receipts are accounted for in a complete and timely manner. Prompt accounting for receipts prevents the temporary use of cash for private purposes before the recording of its receipt. This type of temporary 'borrowing' by employees entails a considerable risk that the business may lose the money.

A business should incorporate the following measures within its procedure for cash receipts.

- The cashier should see signed receipts before he accepts the money from a collector. An exception arises where the cashier is on the cash desk as it is he who will hand in the receipt. Also, it is not normal to give a receipt for money received by post.
- Consecutively numbered receipts, signed by an authorised person (not the collector, cashier or credit-control desk) should be recorded in the books of accounts.
- Receipts should be so designed that they are difficult to forge and the debtor should be made aware of the importance of a receipt when he makes a payment.
- The cash-received book (or similar register) should contain a record including the debtor's name, amount and date received, and initials confirming that the receipt is made out in accordance with data recorded in the cash-received book.
- When cash collection is carried out by a collector he should sign the initialled receipts and, if he has banked the money, paying-in slips.
- He should hand over all amounts received but not banked, and uncollected debts to the cashier. The collector should note uncollected debts which should be passed to the credit-control function.
- Debt settlements in the form of cheques or cash can be received either by post, through collectors or the cashier. Where money is received by post, procedures should be in place to ensure that all mail is opened by two clerks, one of whom records the receipt of the money while the other initials the entry as being accurate. The cheques should then be handed to the cashier who enters them in the cash book and arranges timely delivery to the bank. Cheques received by the collector or cashier should be treated in the same manner as cash receipts.

Controlling Cash Payments

Cash payments should only be made on the receipt of a duly authorised document, for example a cheque requisition, expense claim form, petty-cash advance form, etc. The document should clearly show the amount, authorising signature and payment reference, and date.

The authorising signatory should be made responsible for ensuring the necessary controls have been applied. The payment document should normally be accompanied by adequate, documented evidence – such as an invoice – so that the signatory can verify that the payment is justified. Where the volume of transactions for authorisation is large and the provision of documentation for each payment is impractical, the signatory should spot check the documentation on a random basis. Full documentation should be inspected where payments are over a certain amount. Different levels of authorised signatory should be required depending on the responsibility for the expenditure and the amount involved. When making a cash payment the cashier should normally have this confirmed by the recipient's signature.

On payment, cash documents should be stamped with a dated 'Paid' stamp to prevent them from being presented for payment twice.

Example 4 *Cash control checklist*

1. Is there adequate segregation of duties in all areas where cash is handled?
2. Are adequate safeguards present for ensuring all remittances received by post reach the cashier without delay?
3. Are there adequate procedures for recording cash and cheques received?
4. Are all cash receipts banked each day?
5. Are official receipts issued for all payments?
6. Does the cashier ever issue temporary receipts?
7. Is the total cash banked and the total amount of receipts regularly checked against each other?
8. Are paying-in slips completed by the cashier when he pays in cash at the bank?
9. Does the bank stamp or does the duplicate of the paying-in slip indicate that money has been banked?
10. Is a bank reconciliation statement prepared at least once a month? And is it checked by an independent officer?

11. Does the cashier make entries in the ledger?
12. Are cheques used for paying out all significant amounts?
13. Are cheque books kept safely and in the custody of an appropriate person?
14. Is the imprest system used for controlling petty cash?
15. Are cheques signed only by authorised personnel?
16. Are signatories and signing limits laid down in a written procedure?
17. Are petty-cash vouchers authorised?
18. Is a frequent but irregular check made on the balance of cash kept by the cashier?
19. Are facilities and procedures for the security of cash and cheques adequate?
20. How often are independent checks made on the cash office and control procedures?
21. Have previous recommendations for improvement been implemented?

Authorised cheque signatories should be notified to the business' bankers and should be restricted to as few in number as is practicable. Cheques must be prenumbered for control purposes and crossed ensuring that they can only be paid through a bank account. Used cheques should be entered in a register for future reference.

Control

An independent check should be carried out from time to time to ascertain the effectiveness of a business internal control over cash and bank accounts. An internal control checklist should be prepared and completed regularly, as in Example 4. It should be noted that the checklist shown is illustrative only. More detailed questions can be formulated and many businesses prefer to separately check the cash payments, cash receipts and petty-cash system. Any weaknesses revealed in the systems should be investigated and remedied as soon as possible to prevent possible fraud or errors occurring.

5

Cashflow Forecasts

A business must have the cash it needs to meet its day-to-day commitments, such as the payment of suppliers and employees. It should not have too much cash as the surplus could be used to reduce any overdrafts or be invested elsewhere. Therefore, the business needs to anticipate its cash shortages or surpluses in order to take effective action in good time. This gives rise to the need for cash forecasting.

Producing Forecasts

There are essentially two bases upon which a cashflow forecast can be produced:

- Receipts and payments basis; or
- A balance sheet basis.

The receipts and payments method of forecasting is particularly useful in the short term for identifying peaks and troughs in the business' cash position. Where a deficit is anticipated the forecast should lead to short-term actions, such as arranging appropriate overdraft facilities or the delaying of expenditure. Surpluses above a certain level should signal to a business an opportunity for short-term investments through money market dealings. It is essential that a business uses the forecast to ensure that cash shortages are covered so that claims against the business can be discharged. It has been known for potentially profitable and even profitable businesses to go into liquidation because arrangements have not been made to finance short-term liquidity problems.

By using the forecast receipts and payments a business will be able to consider the appropriateness of its proposed actions. Major acquisitions of fixed assets may have to be postponed, or policies concerning stock levels and credit periods may have to be revised in the light of the forecast cash position.

The balance-sheet method, or source and application of funds statement, is generally more suitable when forecasting over a longer time period. It is particularly useful for deciding financing strategy. The type of long-term finance, whether by a rights issue, raising new equity, the arrangement of leasing or loan finance could be indicated by the forecast. The simplified funds flow statement shown in Table 5.1 may have to be augmented by appropriate levels of detailed information for this purpose.

Table 5.1 *Comparison of cashflow forecast methods*

Cashflow Receipts and Payments Method				Cashflow Balance-Sheet Method			
	Jan	Feb	Mar		Apr	May	June
B/fwd cash	—	—	—	B/fwd cash	—	—	—
Receipts				Sources of funds			
from debtors	—	—	—	profit	—	—	—
others	—	—	—	depreciation	—	—	—
Payments				Application of funds			
to creditors	—	—	—	fixed assets	—	—	—
salaries	—	—	—	working capital	—	—	—
others	—	—	—	others	—	—	—
	═	═	═		═	═	═
C/fwd cash	═	═	═	C/fwd cash	═	═	═

The method of forecasting used will depend upon the circumstances, and it is not uncommon to find a business using both. The differences between the two methods can readily be identified in Table 5.1.

Both methods exclude non-cash items; so it is common in the balance-sheet method to identify separately items such as depreciation, stock obsolescence and bad-debt provision. The depreciation charge is added back to the profit figure and is normally shown as a source of funds.

Accuracy and assumptions

The usefulness of cashflow forecasts depends largely upon their accuracy. A business should constantly review the assumptions upon which forecasts are made and test the forecast against actual outcomes in order to identify and rectify forecasting weaknesses. Sensitivity analysis should be used where appropriate, and a business should generally adopt a conservative view when producing a usable cashflow forecast.

When producing cashflow forecasts the required level of accuracy of the forecast should be determined before carrying out the detailed calculations. A meaningless and misleading forecast is likely if the level of accuracy sought does not take account of the historic volatility of the business and its industrial environment. Accuracy of previous forecasts should be measured and used as a guide to the expected accuracy of future forecasts. Short-term cash forecasting can be improved by comparing actuals with forecasts, particularly when the causes of variances have been fully investigated and explained. An example of this style of presentation is shown in the cash statement in Table 5.2.

The forecasts should be structured around the key variables in the business performance. As the future can only be guessed at, assumptions have to be made. But whatever assumptions are made when producing a forecast these should be clearly stated so that users of the forecast are aware of its basis.

Most businesses start with the obvious assumptions such as sales, profit margins and credit periods taken. The next set of

Table 5.2 *Cash statement*

Cash Statement

	Actual	Forecast	Variance	Next Week Forecast
Receipts				
Payments				
.				
Net cashflow				
B/fwd cash				
C/fwd cash				
Unpresented cheques				
Bank balance				

assumptions relate to production, stockholding and time taken to pay suppliers. Other assumptions regarding the key variables should also be stated but should be kept to the minimum necessary to produce a meaningful forecast.

Assumptions affecting the external environment in which the business trades should not be overlooked. Fluctuations in interest rates, exchange rates and inflation can significantly affect a business income and profitability, and a view as to their movement over the forecast period should be formed and stated.

Assumptions should be critically reviewed when the cashflow forecast has been produced and should be updated when revising forecasts. The critical review, which often leads to a revision of the assumptions, should consider the attainability, sensitivity and reasonableness of the assumptions made.

Cash receipts

The anticipated level of sales is vital to the accuracy of a cashflow forecast. Some aspects of sales forecasts were discussed in relation to stock control in Chapter 3 indicating the importance of sales forecasts in working-capital management.

The choice of method to use when forecasting sales is influenced by a number of factors including the nature of the product, method of distribution, size of the business and degree of competition. A business will obtain the most accurate forecast by employing a combination of the six methods available, both subjective and statistical, which are outlined below.

1. Opinions of salesforce

Salesmen and sales managers can usefully contribute to the production of a sales forecast by applying their subjective judgement of future demand. In the short term such judgements prove to be fairly reliable. Salesmen can often provide reliable forecasts on existing product lines but should not be asked to give estimates of sales of new products which have not been marketed before.

2. Forward orders

In certain industries, particularly heavy engineering, military defence and medical systems, it is common for some, or even all sales to be the result of previously placed orders. Where a full order book exists, sales forecasting should be simple. In other instances the forward orders should be incorporated into the forecast along with an estimate of further orders and a forecast of off-the-shelf sales.

3. Market research

Forecasting future sales involves determining the demand for the business products. This requires determining the total demand for the products and the proportion, or market share, which the business can expect. The data upon which demand forecasts can be made may be collected in a variety of ways.

Outside specialists are often employed to collect and analyse relevant data. There are a number of techniques used for such analysis including the use of questionnaires, test sampling particular groups or observing customers' purchasing patterns.

4. Statistical techniques

Statistical techniques are often used to supplement the other methods of forecasting sales. The two main categories of statistical technique used in sales forecasting are time series and regression analysis.

Time-series models. These make use of historical data. A trend is established which is based on past sales history. This is then projected for the future using the relationship established between past sales and time. As the past can *only* be a guide to the future, the time-series based forecasts should only be considered a guide to the expected level of sales over the forecast period.

The three major time-series methods are:

- Trend fitting – sales data is tested to see if it conforms to a relationship in the form of a particular type of curve, such as exponential, polynomial or logistic. If a curve does fit the data it is extrapolated into the future.
- Moving average – as with the above method, recordings of past sales are plotted. The difference is that an average of the data is used which results in a smoother trend. This, to an extent, tends to eliminate erratic data.
- Exponential smoothing – a moving average of past data is taken. This is then biased towards the more recent data. Recent sales are given a higher weighting than previous sales.

Regression analysis, or econometric modelling. This uses past data to derive a model by testing likely relationships between variables until a statistically satisfactory 'fit' is found. The sales which are being forecast are termed the dependent variable.

These are tested to find the relationship between itself and the independent variables, such as competitors' prices, distribution channels, advertising expenditure and economic growth.

This type of model can be tested for a level of significance, or its forecasting ability. Sensitivity analysis is easily applied, providing more information for decision-making than time-series methods. It is useful for ascertaining major turning points and for forecasting the probable impact of a change in any of the variables affecting demand.

Many software packages incorporating statistical facilities are readily available for use with microcomputers. Standard spreadsheet packages, such as Lotus 1–2–3 and Supercalc, contain statistical functions which are powerful easy-to-use tools for sales forecasting. The available functions include the calculation of moving averages, exponential smoothing and linear regression.

It should be emphasised that a business will obtain the most accurate forecast of sales by employing a combination of techniques, both statistical and subjective. One consumer goods distributor, for example, produces sales forecasts using salesmens' and regional sales managers' judgements which incorporate their commitment to achieving future sales targets. These judgements are reviewed in the light of forecasts based on statistical techniques (using Lotus 1–2–3 facilities). Agreement on the sales forecast is made, once these inputs have been considered against the forecast economic indicators (exchange rates, interest rate and inflation) provided by the treasury department.

Once a sales forecast has been made the business must then estimate the amount and timing of the future cash receipts. The levels of cash sales, credit sales, discounts and bad debts should be applied along with the expected (which is likely to be different to the agreed) credit term.

Other cash receipts expected in the forecast period must also be included. Items commonly found in this category are interest or dividends receivable from trade or other investments, and receipts from the sale of fixed assets or even from the disposal of part of the business.

| | JANUARY | | | | FEBRUARY | | | | MARCH | | | | (and so on) |
	Week 1	Week 2	Week 3	Week 4	Week 1	Week 2	Week 3	Week 4	Week 1	Week 2	Week 3	Week 4	
Cash balance B/F													
Receipts													
Sales £													
DM													
$													
Yen													
Other													
Investments													
Asset sales													
Other													
Total receipts													
Payments													
Purchases £													
DM													
$													
Yen													
Other													
Salaries													
Other operating expenses													
Tax													
Dividends and interest													
Capital expenditure													
Other													
Total payments													
Net receipts payments													
Cash balance													

Note: This weekly/monthly forecast is drawn up for twelve months.

Figure 5.3 Cashflow forecast

5. Cash payments

From the sales forecast and assumptions of the levels of stock a business will hold, a production forecast can be made. This determines the required purchases of raw materials. By applying assumptions regarding lead times and payment terms, a business can then forecast its cash outflows on purchased goods.

Other operating expenses such as wages, national insurance, pensions, electricity and gas can usually be forecast with a good deal of accuracy, as can fixed overheads such as rates, rental of equipment and salaries. The cash payments for these items should be included in the cash forecast as should irregular payments such as corporation tax, dividends and major asset purchases (machinery, equipment, land or buildings).

Net cashflow

The cash receipts and payments are shown in the forecast statement on a period-by-period basis. The choice of period – weeks, months or quarters – will depend on the nature and variability of the cashflows. The net of receipts and payments is added to the initial cash balance to provide the balances at the end of each period.

Some businesses with significant foreign currency payments, and/or receipts, include this information, converted to the anticipated sterling equivalent, in the cashflow forecast statement. Other businesses may wish to use the forecast for a number of purposes including short and longer-term funding or investment decisions. **Figure 5.3** illustrates the possibilities of incorporating such information within the one cashflow forecast.

Resolving Cashflow Problems

When a cashflow forecast has been made a business can identify the cashflow problems which it will have to resolve. If the forecast indicates *short-term* cash shortages with an overall satisfactory balance then the following procedure should be taken up.

- Review each item in the forecast regarding its timing and amount (this is where the assumptions about credit terms would be reviewed).
- Reduce or re-phase the amount of the proposed expenditure. It is important that expenditure is classified as discretionary or essential so that only discretionary items are reduced or eliminated.
- Review safety stock levels (this has implications for the order level).
- Review debt collection procedures.
- Arrange for short-term overdraft facilities or obtain other short-term forms of finance.

If the forecast highlights short-term surpluses then short-term investments (see Chapter 8) should be made. If longer-term shortages are indicated it is necessary for the business to obtain long-term finance in the form of capital or loans (also Chapter 8). If the forecast identifies long-term surpluses (not just seasonal peaks) the business should look for opportunities to expand its business or invest the surplus in other businesses.

6

Bank Account Management

Previous chapters have explained the actions which can be taken within a business to manage liquidity effectively. This is the first of four chapters which will examine how the external activities of the business can also affect cashflow. In this particular chapter we discover how the prudent management of bank accounts can result in cost savings for a business. However, before any consideration of how a business can get the best from its banks, it is necessary to understand the basic operations of the UK clearing process.

The Clearing Process

The process of making a payment involves debiting the payer's bank account and crediting the payee's bank account. When a payment is made through the banking system, there are three different situations which can apply.

- Both payer and payee hold accounts at the same bank branch.
- Both payer and payee hold accounts at the same bank, but at different branches.
- Payer and payee hold accounts at different banks.

The methods of transfer used by the banks are different in each case. When payer and payee both hold accounts at the same bank branch, the transfer is made for same-day value within the branch. That is, the payer's account is debited and the payee's account credited on the day that payment instructions are given. In the situation where payer and payee both hold accounts at different branches of the same bank, the transfer is made within that bank's internal system, normally with a one or two day value delay. However, in the case where payer and payee hold accounts at different banks, the clearing system comes into operation.

Clearing is the process of sorting out all the payments which have been input into the banking system to arrange debit and credit entries to be passed to the correct bank accounts. In the UK the old idea of clearing banks has become obsolete as there are now different clearing organisations for different types of payment. The member banks of these organisations operate the clearing process for the particular type of payment. If non-member banks wish to process payments they must be passed through member banks for clearing.

The high-volume paper clearing (mostly cheques and standing orders) is the responsibility of The Cheque and Credit Clearing Company. The members of this organisation are:

- Bank of England
- Bank of Scotland
- Barclays Bank
- Co-operative Bank
- Girobank
- Lloyds Bank
- Midland Bank
- National Westminster Bank
- The Royal Bank of Scotland
- Trustee Savings Bank

The clearing of large transfers to be made for value the same day, such as CHAPS or other automatic transfers, is the responsibility of the CHAPS and Town Clearing Company. The members of this organisation are:

- Bank of England
- Bank of Scotland
- Barclays Bank
- Citibank

- Clydesdale Bank
- Co-operative Bank
- Coutts & Co
- Girobank
- Lloyds Bank
- Midland Bank
- National Westminster Bank
- The Royal Bank of Scotland
- Standard Chartered Bank
- Trustee Savings Bank

In the UK, the standard time taken for clearing cheques is three business days. This means that if a business deposits a cheque with its bank on Thursday, then funds will be received in the business' account on the following Tuesday. The principal exception to this rule is the town clearing cheque. This is a cheque drawn on a bank located in the City of London. Town cheques can be identified by the letter 'T' in the sorting code and, provided they are deposited in another bank account in the City of London, same day value will be received.

Bank Balance Information

In order to manage a bank account efficiently, it is necessary to receive regular balance information either by mail, telephone or via a computer link. The three different methods of receiving bank-balance information are discussed below.

1. *Bank statements.* A bank statement is a written report of movements on a bank account over a given period. The statement shows an opening balance, itemises all debits and credits and gives a closing balance for the end of the period. Bank statements can be obtained quarterly, monthly, weekly or daily, on request. Daily statements are practical for an active bank account but these should be backed up by monthly statements as a double check that all items have been included. For accounts which do not have frequent movements, weekly statements are sufficient.

It is important to remember that the balance shown on a bank statement is normally the bank's book or ledger balance. This is because the bank credits its customers' accounts as soon as an incoming cheque is paid into the banking system, which is usually before clearance takes place. During the clearing period, the bank has credited the payee's ledger balance, but cannot give 'good value' on the funds. That is, the funds are not available to be used by the payee and the payee would not be permitted to draw the funds out as cash.

The cheque clearance process can result in the company and the bank recording three different account balances for the same account:

- Cash-book balance which credits cheques received by the company but not yet recorded by the bank.
- Bank-ledger balance which credits cheques lodged with the bank but not cleared.
- Bank-cleared balance which takes account of the clearing process and represents the true position between the company and the bank. This is the figure which counts against overdraft and loan facility limits.

Most banks now have the ability to convert automatically ledger balances into cleared balances, so providing statements giving cleared balances. However, this is something which must be specifically requested by the customer.

2. *Telephone information.* Most banks will provide balance information over the telephone if this service is requested in writing in advance. The most current balance information is given over the telephone which can be used as a supplement to bank statements. Typical details which might be given are:

- Last night's cleared balance.
- This morning's opening-cleared balance.
- Items expected to clear today.
- Tonight's forecast closing balance.

The bank calculates the forecast closing balance by adjusting the opening-cleared balance for items in clearing as shown in the example below.

Table 6.1

	Tuesday 2 June £
Last night's cleared balance	184,890
Items clearing overnight	5,670
This morning's opening-cleared balance	190,560
Items expected to clear today	(72,000)
Tonight's forecast closing balance	118,560

This forecast is by no means a foolproof figure as debits and credits, which are not passed through the clearing process, may also affect the account balance.

3. *Electronic balance reporting.* Bank balance information can be received automatically via a computer terminal and telephone link. Most banks market an electronic balance-reporting service and can provide cleared or ledger balances, detailed credit and debit information and forecast balances. In the UK the major banks have reached agreement that they will input information to the other banks' balance-reporting services. This means that businesses which use more than one bank can obtain all their balance information from the same terminal in a uniform format.

The advantage of electronic balance-reporting is the convenience of having preformatted reports available first thing in the morning without having to contact the bank directly. Unfortunately, the major drawback of these services is their high cost which puts them beyond the scope of many businesses.

Bank Charges

As all businesses use essentially the same banking services, it seems surprising that some pay higher bank charges than others.

The reason is that some businesses are more attractive clients to a bank than others. Banks will compete for the business of major organisations but with smaller customers the banks are not so eager and these businesses are in a much weaker bargaining position. The types of business which are attractive banking clients are those which are:

- Highly credit worthy.
- Major corporations or household names.
- Likely to buy a range of other banking services such as merchant banking or trade finance.
- In a growth industry.
- Rapidly expanding within a market sector.
- Likely to be the subject of a takeover from a major organisation.

Bank charges are a great cause for concern for many businesses and a frequent worry is whether the business is paying higher bank charges than its competitors. There are two ways in which businesses can pay for their banking services.

1. On a per item basis.
2. By leaving an idle credit balance in the account.

When charges are paid on an itemised basis the business may feel more burdened with checking the individual charges, but at least it knows the true cost of its banking services. This enables it to undertake informed bargaining with the bank when it attempts to reduce the cost of particular services. The disadvantage of payment with idle balance is that it masks the true cost of banking services.

It is difficult for businesses to bargain with banks over charges when they do not know the relative cost-effectiveness of their own banking services. Businesses are generally very secretive about their bank charges as they wish to avoid this information being passed to their competitors. However, less secrecy exists between businesses which are not competitors and it may be possible for managers to discuss bank charges with the representatives of other businesses. The opportunity to meet such individuals sometimes exists through trade associations, professional bodies and Chambers of Commerce.

Another way of reducing bank charges is to introduce a competitive element in banking services. Some businesses go so far as putting their banking services out to tender and invite several banks to compete for the business. When banks are eager to gain new clients or to retain an existing account they will offer their most attractive rates to the business. This competitive approach to banking services can only be used by firms which are seen by the banks as a desirable client. Companies which have had to call upon their banks for help in times of crisis cannot expect fierce competition for their business.

Different Types of Bank Account

There are a number of different types of bank account which a business can use to manage cash.

In general, all bank accounts provide a short-term means of holding cash and some accounts also offer loan (overdraft) facilities. Accounts vary largely in terms of the interest which is paid for credit balances, the currency in which the account is held and the terms under which funds can be withdrawn.

Current accounts

A current account is the most liquid type of bank account as funds are available for immediate withdrawal from the account once they have cleared. Current accounts are not normally interest bearing, but interest may be charged by the bank if the account balance becomes a debit position (an overdrawn balance). Cheque books are normally available for current accounts upon request. This type of account lends itself to trading use and most businesses of all sizes hold at least one current account.

Deposit accounts

Deposit accounts differ from current accounts as they are interest bearing. As discussed elsewhere in this chapter, it is important that large credit balances are transferred to deposit accounts and are not allowed to accumulate in current accounts. Deposit accounts can, in some cases, be less liquid than current accounts as it may be necessary to give notice of the intention to withdraw funds.

Currency accounts

In this chapter we have considered the operation of bank accounts denominated in the base currency, in this case sterling. However, many businesses have significant interests in other currencies and find it necessary to hold currency accounts. Both current and deposit accounts can be held in the UK, denominated in all the major traded currencies, and can be operated in exactly the same way as sterling accounts. The business can make payments, issue cheques and receive funds in currency using a currency current account. However, it is important to remember that all balances on currency accounts, both debit and credit, represent a currency exposure to the business. This means that the business will make gains or losses due to movements in the exchange rate as a result of holding a net shortage or surplus of currency.

Multi-currency accounts

A business which does not have sufficient business in a particular currency to warrant holding a currency account may choose to hold a multi-currency account. This is an account denominated in the base currency and requested by the business but which can be used to make payments or to collect funds in a number of other currencies. The currency conversions are made by the bank, normally at a daily exchange rate ruling on the value date. A business which operates a multi-currency account will have cheques which are blank in both currency and amount, and which can be used to make payments in any of the major traded currencies. The statement of account will show both amounts and currencies as shown in Table 6.2.

Table 6.2 *A multi-currency bank statement*

Transaction	Type	Value date	£
Opening Balance			250,000
Sw Fr 500,0007 2.5000	Receipt	26.06.8X	200,000
DM 5,000,0007 3.0000	Payment	26.06.8X	(1,666,667)
US$ 800,0007 1.6000	Receipt	27.06.8X	500,000
Yen 250,000,0007 250.00	Receipt	30.06.8X	1,000,000
Fr Fr 450,0007 6.0000	Payment	01.07.8X	(75,000)
Closing balance			208,333

Currency transactions without a currency account

A business which does not have sufficient volume of currency transactions to make a currency bank account worthwhile, may still occasionally receive a currency cheque or need to make a currency payment. It is possible to pay currency cheques into a sterling bank account, although the clearing time may be quite long and the bank charges can be high. The bank will make the currency exchange at a rate ruling on the value date. To make currency payments without a currency account it is possible to ask the bank to draw up a foreign currency draft, although the charges for this can also be quite high.

Bank Balance Management

The aim of bank balance management is to maximise the interest income of a business and to minimise interest costs. There are three fundamental principles which a business must observe.

1. The business must always be aware of its current position with the bank. It is impossible to control the costs of banking

services without this knowledge.

2. Significant credit balances must never be allowed to remain in non-interest-bearing current accounts.

3. Overdraft usage must be carefully monitored to ensure that the business is not paying overdraft interest rates for funds which could be borrowed more cheaply elsewhere.

Bank Overdrafts

An overdraft (loan) facility is sometimes available for current accounts, enabling businesses to move from credit to debit. Overdraft facilities are only available upon permission from the bank manager. In order to obtain this permission, the business must present its case for the facility and explain the proposed repayment schedule.

The interest charge for an overdraft account is normally based on a fixed percentage rate over the bank's base rate. This rate will vary according to the perceived credit-worthiness of the business. Overdrafts provide businesses with the flexibility to cope with occasional cash shortages. A business which identifies a need for a medium or long-term cash injection would be best advised to approach its bank for a negotiated loan.

Performing bank account reconciliations

It is important for a business to keep up to date with its position at the bank, and for this reason regular bank account reconciliations are essential. This process has been covered in previous chapters of this book.

Using deposit accounts

The simplest way of ensuring that funds do not lie idle in current accounts is to calculate a forecast closing balance each day. If the account has a significant credit balance, transfer the balance to a deposit account held with the same bank. This transfer can be arranged over the telephone and confirmed in writing afterwards using a standard letter. An example letter is shown below.

Example 5 *Letter to transfer funds from a current to deposit account.*

2 October 198X

The Manager
XYZ Bank
30 High Street
Willington WR10 1SJ
Dear Sir,

Re: Current account number 12345678

This is to confirm our telephone conversation of today, in which we requested you to transfer the sum of £........ to our deposit account number 87654321, held with yourselves, with immediate effect.

Yours faithfully,

Authorised signatory

A forecast closing balance can be calculated by taking the forecast balance provided by the bank and making adjustments for any items known to the business which are not being processed through the normal clearing system. Such items include same-day electronic transfers, town or 'special' cleared cheques, and cash deposits.

It is quite simple to calculate the minimum value of funds which warrant transfer to the deposit account by conducting a simple cost/benefit analysis. The costs to consider are the bank charges made for the transfer and a notional internal charge for administration. For example, if the total cost of the transfer is presumed to be £8, then a transfer is worthwhile when the interest earned exceeds £8.

If interest rates are 10 per cent then the breakeven calculation is:

$$\frac{10\% \times £z}{365} = £8 \text{ or } £z = £8 \times 365 \times \frac{100}{10}$$

Therefore the breakeven amount is £29,200.

Clearly, it is not worthwhile depositing funds if the principal amount is only slightly greater than the breakeven amount. In the above case, the business might make a rule to deposit amounts over £50,000 whilst interest rates remained at the same level.

Money-market borrowing

If a business has a net shortage of funds, it may be possible to borrow more cheaply by using money market dealings than through overdraft accounts. In the money market only sizeable deals are traded. The actual minimum amount depends upon the individual bank concerned but amounts of £100,000 upwards are normal. In order to borrow in the money markets a business must establish a loan facility with one or more banks and ensure that staff are trained to deal. Aspects of money market dealing are dealt with in a later chapter of this book.

Pooling Systems

When a business operates more than one bank account, it is a fundamental rule that it should never be overdrawn on one account whilst another account is in credit. This is because, even at the finest interest rates, there will always be a margin between the deposit and borrowing interest rates. Thus, if the bank is lending money at 10 per cent then it will only be paying 9.5 per cent for deposits. A business which is both a borrower and a lender would therefore make a net loss of 0.5 per cent.

The solution is for the business to lend to itself so that dealings with the bank are reduced and interest costs are minimised. This process is known as 'pooling'. An example is provided in the following diagram where three subsidiaries each operate their own current accounts with the bank.

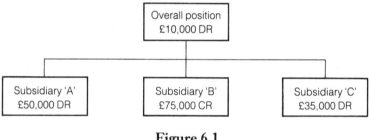

Figure 6.1

There is a net overdrawn position of £10,000 at the end of the day, whereas without pooling the company would have been borrowing £85,000 on overdraft and depositing £75,000 with resultant interest losses.

The simplest way for a business to operate a pooling system is to make arrangements with the bank so that they do all the administrative work. In the UK, pooling can be operated by all the major banks and it is necessary for the business to enter into a contract with the bank for these services to be provided. All the accounts for inclusion have to be held with the same bank, but not necessarily the same branch.

The net balance on the pooled accounts would be notified to the business each day either by a telephone call from the bank or via an electronic balance reporting system.

The bank will operate the pooling system in one of two ways:

1. Notional offset for interest purposes only. The account balances are left unchanged by the pooling system, but the bank nets the balances in its own books and only charges interest on the net overdrawn position.
2. Actual movements between the accounts. The bank adjusts the account balances to show the pooling processing operation.

The balances are either adjusted to zero ('zero balancing') or to some target figure previously agreed by the business ('target balancing').

The different pooling mechanisms are illustrated below.

Table 6.3 *Notional offset*

	Forecast closing balances £
Subsidiary 'A' account	100,000 DR
Subsidiary 'B' account	250,000 CR
Subsidiary 'C' account	30,000 DR
Amount available for transfer to a deposit account	120,000 CR

In the above example the business would withdraw £120,000 from the main account (say, account 'D') making the balance on that account overdrawn. The net balance on all the accounts would then be zero. The business would not be charged for the overdraft on account 'D' as this would be offset by credit balances on the other accounts.

Table 6.4 *Zero balancing*

	Forecasting closing balances £	Transfer in/(out)
Subsidiary 'A' account	100,000 DR	100,000
Subsidiary 'B' account	250,000 CR	(250,000)
Subsidiary 'C' account	30,000 DR	30,000
Net transfer to main account		(120,000)

Under a system of zero balancing, the ledger balances of all the subsidiary accounts are changed to zero at the end of each day. This is done by transfers to and from the main account (account 'D'). As before, a credit balance on account 'D' would then be transferred to a deposit account.

Table 6.5 *Target balancing*

	Forecasting closing balances £	*Transfer in/(out)*
Subsidiary 'A' account	100,000 DR	120,000
Subsidiary 'B' account	250,000 CR	(230,000)
Subsidiary 'C' account	30,000 DR	50,000
Net transfer to main account		(60,000)

In some cases, the business does not want all the account balances to be changed to zero. This often occurs when the business remunerates its banks by means of agreed idle balances. In the example shown above, the company leaves a credit balance of £20,000 on each account resulting in a smaller transfer to account 'D'. The credit balance on account 'D' would then be transferred to a deposit account as before.

Interest charges for pooling

Interest costs incurred on overdrawn balances resulting from pooling systems are normally charged on the main account. When the pooled accounts belong to different subsidiary companies or divisions, most businesses also operate some internal system of interest apportionment between the various participating accounts. This is normally done by paying interest on credit balances and charging on interest on overdrafts. It is important to understand that these interest entries are made using the funds of the business, not the bank. The rate used for internal interest charging is decided by the business and is usually the same for borrowings or deposits within the pool. It is common to use a market rate such as the bank's base rate. Interest adjustments can either be made by the bank, on behalf of the business, or transferred within the business through the internal intercompany ledger accounts.

Pooling accounts in foreign currencies

This chapter has considered pooling for sterling bank accounts held in the UK. However, many businesses have several accounts denominated in a foreign currency and wish to save costs by pooling. The possibilities for pooling foreign currency accounts are largely determined by the currency in question and whether the accounts are held in the UK or overseas.

1. Currency accounts held in the UK can be pooled together in the same way as sterling accounts, provided the bank is prepared to accommodate this. In practice, there are no problems in pooling accounts held in the normal trading currencies.
2. Currency accounts held overseas can be pooled together providing this is permitted by the regulatory bodies in the country in question. Another limiting factor for overseas pooling is that the banking systems in some countries are not sufficiently sophisticated to meet the information requirements of a pooling system.

It is possible to operate pooling systems across national boundaries and some companies use this technique, for example, to pool their US dollar accounts in Europe. The opportunities for cross-border pooling are dependent on the absence of exchange controls and the existence of on-line information systems to provide current data on overseas balances.

As with any other foreign-currency bank account, it is important to remember that net balances on pooled accounts (both debit and credit) represent a currency exposure for the business.

7

Transferring Cash

All businesses need to make and receive cash transfers in order to carry out their trade, and there are a range of different techniques which can be used to transfer cash from one party to another. Each of these techniques is best suited to particular businesses or types of transaction.

Chapter 1 showed the importance of using the correct cash-transfer instruments as a means of managing the cash collection and payment cycles. For the cash-collection cycle, the business aims to receive value for funds at the earliest possible time; for the cash-payments cycle, the business wishes to retain value for the funds until the latest possible time. Thus, a business will generally aim to use the fastest transfer techniques for collections and the slowest for payments.

Transfer Techniques

The principal manual transfer techniques are cash, cheques, drafts, bank-to-bank transfers, direct debits, standing orders and credit cards. In addition, there are computerised techniques, such as Electronic Funds Transfers (EFT), Bankers Automated Clearing System (BACS) and Clearing House Automated Payments System (CHAPS).

Cash

Cash takes the form of notes and coins and is commonly used for smaller transactions such as retail purchases. Cash is the most liquid type of payment since it is not normally the subject of clearing. However, if cash is deposited into a bank branch other than that at which the account is held, there will be a delay resulting from the branch clearing. The use of cash eliminates any credit risk on payments as value for the transfer rests with the party which holds the cash. Thus, cash is the original 'bearer instrument'. The greatest drawback of using cash for transactions is the high cost of providing adequate security and correct handling procedures.

Cheques

A cheque is a set of written payment instructions to debit an account held at the bank to which the instructions are addressed. The standard clearing time for cheques in the UK is three working days. Thus, a cheque deposited with the bank on Thursday morning will be cleared by the following Tuesday morning. Major banking customers can frequently negotiate with their banks to receive two days' value for cheque clearing. Cheques are frequently used for business and retail transactions and as the payee is specified on the face of the cheque, they are not subject to the same security risks as cash.

Drafts

The term draft is used to cover a variety of financial instruments which are traded on the money markets of the world. In the UK a draft is normally taken to mean a banker's draft which is a set of payment instructions similar to a cheque, drafted by the bank rather than by the payer. The advantage of the payment being drafted by the bank is that the bank ensures that the payer's account can cover the value of the draft.

Drafts are quite costly compared to other means of cash transfer and they have to be ordered from the bank in advance of their use. Their use is generally limited to occasions when a paper transfer is required but funds must be guaranteed, thereby ruling out the use of a cheque. If requested, a draft can be backed by a bank guarantee so that the credit risk is that of the bank, rather than the payer. The inclusion of a bank guarantee increases the cost of the draft.

Bank-to-bank transfers

A bank-to-bank transfer takes place when money is remitted from one bank account to another through the banker's internal transfer systems. A transfer will be initiated upon receipt by the bank of either written, verbal or electronic instructions from the payer. Written instructions are given by means of mail, telex or telegraphic ('wire') messages; verbal instructions are given over the telephone (although this is generally followed by a written confirmation) and electronic instructions are given via a computer link.

The payer's involvement with the transfer ceases once payment instructions have been passed to the bank. Internally the bank may carry out the instructions using banking systems such as CHAPS or BACS which are discussed later in this section.

Direct debits

Direct debits are payment requests submitted to the payer's bank by the payee which enable approved creditors to debit the bank accounts of their debtors directly. Direct debits are normally used for domestic purposes, such as payment of rates and other bills, but they can also be used for trade payments. The disadvantage of direct debits for trade purposes is the fact that, as the payments are not initiated by the payer, an element of control is lost. In order to arrange a direct debit transfer, the payer must give advance authorisation to its bank to honour the payee's request, provided certain conditions are met. Clearance of direct debit transfers normally takes two business days, but same-day value can be achieved by submitting the debits to the bank ahead of the due date.

Standing orders

Standing orders are written payment instructions in which a payer requests the bank to meet regular payments to the same payee, for the same amount and on the same day of each month. Payments resulting from standing order instructions cease only upon further instructions from the payer to the bank. Standing orders are most commonly used for monthly or weekly payments, such as rental, hire purchase or lease instalments.

Credit cards

Credit cards are normally used as payment only in retail transactions. In a credit-card transaction, the payer owns a uniquely identified secure card which can be used to log charges for goods or services. At the end of each account period, the bank or company which issues the card presents a statement to the card holder for payment. The card holder can either settle the account in full or pay a minimum balance. If the card holder pays less than the full amount, interest will be charged on the balance. With charge cards, which are similar to credit cards, the balance must always be paid in full. Thus, items do not have to be paid for at the time of purchase; instead there is a credit period before the debtor pays. However, there is usually a regular charge to the card holder to cover the cost of credit.

Electronic Funds Transfer (EFT)

These transfers are initiated from instructions fed directly by the customer into a computer link. The use of EFT enables a business to give payment instructions without having to contact the bank directly. The hard copy confirmations for EFT payments are produced immediately by the computer and, once the confirmation is produced, payment is guaranteed by the bank. EFT transfers are normally cheaper than bank-to-bank transfers; however, there is usually a standing charge for the service in addition to the charges for each transfer.

EFT instructions are generally transmitted directly to the payments area of the bank, where they are received by the bank's personnel. The bank then makes the transfer using any appropriate payment method. However, the most efficient computerised payments systems can make payments directly from the customers offices to the payee by automatically activating the bank's internal computerised payments systems.

Clearing House Automated Payments System (CHAPS)

CHAPS was established in 1984 to provide same-day value guaranteed transfers for amounts over £10,000. CHAPS is an automated means of cash transfer which is normally initiated by a bank in order to meet a customer's request for a bank-to-bank transfer. Payments made via CHAPS in the approved manner have the advantages of being irrevocable, unconditional and guaranteed. This means that once the payment has been confirmed by the CHAPS network, the payee has guaranteed receipt of funds.

Instructions for CHAPS payments must be issued over a special CHAPS terminal. It is possible for a business making CHAPS payments to become a CHAPS participant (that is, to have a dedicated CHAPS terminal), instead of accessing CHAPS through a bank. In this case, the administrative costs involved in making payments are reduced as payment instructions can be given without the direct involvement of a bank. However, in most cases the savings are not great enough to warrant the cost of installing a CHAPS terminal which is currently around £7,000. In addition, an annual maintenance charge has to be paid for using the service. Unless a business is making a very large number of payments, it is uneconomic to become a CHAPS participant. For this reason, most corporate users of CHAPS access the CHAPS facilities of their bank by initiating payments with written or telephone instructions.

CHAPS is used to make payments which would previously have been made using telephone/telex transfers. The use of CHAPS is largely invisible to the business which issues payment instructions to the bank, and many businesses are not aware that CHAPS is being used for their transfers. For the bank, the principal benefit of using CHAPS is a reduction in the administration time required for each payment.

Bankers Automated Clearing System (BACS)

BACS is a low-cost funds-transfer system which is particularly suitable for businesses which make a large number of payments at regular intervals. BACS can be used for either debit or credit transfers and is commonly used for salaries and wages, interest and dividend payments.

The mechanism for making BACS payments is for participants to record details of either credit or debit transactions on magnetic tape, cassette or diskettes, and then pass these instructions to a BACS clearing centre for processing. Here the data on the input tape is sorted by a computer to produce an output tape for each bank. These output tapes are then passed back to the relevant banks to be integrated into their own payments systems.

The tapes must be submitted to the clearing centre several days before the value date in order to obtain same-day value for transfers. This lead time means that BACS payments are not suitable for all applications.

In addition to BACS payments initiated by transferring data in 'hard' format, a low-cost alternative is a telecommunications link called BACSTEL which was introduced in 1984. BACSTEL enables data transmission directly from the user to the BACS clearing centre. This is of particular benefit to users located far from the clearing centre who would otherwise suffer time delays when transferring the disks.

The charges for BACS are calculated on the basis of a flat rate for each item processed. The cost of BACS payments is currently between three and four pence per item, which is significantly lower than for cheque or CHAPS transfers.

Cost of Cash Transfers

The manual and computerised transfer techniques discussed above are suited to different purposes because of the various distinguishing features of each. Generally, the cash transfer techniques vary in terms of:

- Cost.
- Speed.
- Security.
- Certainty.

Transfers are normally charged on an itemised basis with the cost of each type of transfer reflecting the speed, security and certainty of the particular mechanism used. In the case of documentary instruments, such as cheques or drafts, a charge is made to cover the administration of the payment and clearing of the instrument. Transfers which are made using the banks' own clearing branch are charged according to individual costs. However, as it is difficult for the banks to establish their own costs, the charges made are an estimated allocation of the overheads plus an appropriate profit margin.

The costs of computerised payment techniques also vary depending upon the features of the particular technique used. For example, BACS transfers have a lower cost than CHAPS but, as BACS cannot be activated for same-day value, they can only be used when same-day value is not required.

Thus, the individual business must select transfer techniques which give speed of transfer, a reasonable level of security and reliability, and all at an acceptable cost. Obviously, different businesses will have various ideas about what is 'reasonable' and 'acceptable' for their purposes, which is why different transfer techniques are used by different businesses.

Delays in Cash Transfer

In order to manage cash effectively, it is important that the most appropriate transfer methods are used for payments and receipts. However, with all cash transfers delays can occur which cause the payee to suffer loss of interest or cost an opportunity of using the funds. One cause of delay occurs when one of the parties acts negligently or deliberately attempts to delay a remittance, but in the normal course of business, delays in the transfer of cash usually result from one of the following causes:

1. Mail delay. This normally occurs only with cheque payments and mail transfers when delays in mailing and delivery enable the payer to have use of the funds for longer. The payer may use

this as a deliberate ploy to maximise available cash by mailing cheques from remote locations.

2. Bank delay. This can occur in bank-to-bank transfers if the paying bank has not been correctly notified of the payee's bank and branch. When transfers become mislaid in the banking system, considerable delays can result with a consequent loss of interest. It is important that payment instructions for the payee's bank account are correctly and accurately given to the payer.

3. Value dating delay. This occurs when value for a payment is not transferred from the payee's bank to the payee at the correct time. Thus it is important to ensure that the correct clearing time is applied to cheques and other receipts. It is surprising how often businesses only presume that they are receiving cheque clearance after three days, without ever checking that this is the case.

4. Advice delay. If the bank does not notify the payee promptly that funds have been received into the account, the payee is prevented from using them. This problem underlines the importance of accurate bank-balance information for cash management.

Improving the Cash Transfer Process

There is a point at which it becomes economic for a business to change its method of cash transfer to improve cash management. In the following example, a company currently receives cheque payments from a customer but can insist upon payment via CHAPS if it will bear the cost of the CHAPS transfer. The company must weigh up the advantages of gaining three days' value on the receivables against the cost of CHAPS. If we assume that the company is paying overdraft interest rates of 10 per cent, then this is the interest cost saving. The cost of a CHAPS transfer is assumed to be £12. The following formula can be used to ascertain the economic break-even amount (X) of a remittance.

$$X = 12 \times \frac{365}{3} \times \frac{100}{10} = £14,600$$

Where:

- The marginal rate of interest to be saved is 10 per cent.
- The number of float days is three.
- The additional cost of CHAPS is £12.

Thus, at overdraft rates of 10 per cent, the cost of supporting an overdraft of £14,600 for three days is £12. This means that for payments in excess of £14,600, the cost of the overdraft would exceed the cost of the CHAPS transfer; it is therefore worthwhile for the company to request CHAPS.

The above formula can be summarised as:

$$X = a \times \frac{365}{b} \times \frac{100}{c}$$

Where:

- a is the additional cost of the alternative payment method.
- b is the number of float days.
- c is the rate of interest cost to be saved.

This example shows that improvements in the cash transfer process can provide real savings to a company. However, as the business is concerned with speeding up receipt of cash and slowing down the disbursement, the actions taken to improve cash transfer are different, depending upon whether the business is acting as the payer or the payee.

The business as payee

In its capacity as payee, the business needs to receive cleared funds at the earliest possible time. The following criteria should be followed.

1. The payment instructions given to the payer must be accurate and complete.

2. It may be worthwhile negotiating with the payer to improve the transfer method. This might involve offering a financial incentive to him, in which case the above formula should be used to establish an appropriate value for such an incentive.

3. For larger businesses it may be possible to negotiate better value dating practices through discussions with the bank.

4. The business should have a fast and efficient system for receiving details of bank balances. This can either involve the telephone or an electronic balance reporting system.

5. It is important to ensure that no delays occur in the business' internal handling procedures for funds received.

The business as payer

As payer the business is concerned with retaining the funds' value until the latest possible time. The payer will use the slowest payment mechanism but must consider the potential damage to its trading relationship if payment is received late by the payee. Accurate bank-balance information is important to the business in its role as payer enabling the appropriate action to be taken when funds value is lost.

Foreign Currency Transfers within the UK

This chapter has so far considered only cash transfers in sterling. However, businesses sometimes need to make transfers in another currency. The cash transfer techniques which are applicable to currency transfers are similar to those used for sterling. For example, cheques and drafts are available in foreign currencies although it is usually necessary to have a currency or multi-currency bank account before drawing a currency cheque. Bank-to-bank transfers can be made in currency and be initiated by either telephone, mail or electronic instructions to the bank. Once again, it is preferable to have a foreign-currency bank account to make these transfers.

International Transfers

Additional complications occur with international currency transfers which can result in delays and consequent losses of interest. Some of the principal factors which affect international funds transfers are:

- The major financial centres exist in different time zones.
- Not all countries benefit from the same level of technology.
- Different countries have variations in business and banking practices.
- Some countries have restrictions on foreign exchange transactions and do not allow the free transfer of funds.

When a business makes payments between different countries, and therefore different banking systems, it must use payment methods which are compatible with those banking systems. The most common techniques for international payments are cheques and electronic bank-to-bank transfers.

Using cheques for international transfers

Many businesses still use cheques for international payments, despite the associated time delays and collection costs. The following example highlights the disadvantages of international cheque collection.

A UK company allows its US customers to settle their accounts by cheques which are mailed to the company in the UK. When the UK company receives these cheque payments they are paid into the UK bank which then has to return the cheques by mail to the US for clearance. Once the cheques have been cleared in the US, the UK is notified that funds are available. Thus, each cheque crosses the Atlantic twice before the UK company receives value for the funds.

The particular problem of collecting cheque payments from the US can be resolved by the use of a 'lockbox' facility, whereby the UK business collects payments in a post office box in the US. A local bank clears the lockbox each day, processes the payments and initiates the clearing mechanism. A lockbox facility can effectively halve the collection time for cheque payments from the US.

Clearing House Interbank Payments System (CHIPS)

In response to the importance of the US dollar as an international currency, a group of New York banks and associates have created a special payments system for US dollars called CHIPS (Clearing House Interbank Payments System). This system has a similar function to the CHAPS system. It involves each payment being designated with a code representing the destination bank, enabling the payment to be processed through the CHIPS network. CHIPS is based in New York and processes over 90 per cent of all US dollar denominated international transactions.

The Society for Worldwide Interbank Financial Telecommunications (SWIFT)

SWIFT is a non-profit making, bank owned, cooperative society which was established in 1973 by 239 banks in 15 countries. SWIFT provides a method of conveying interbank transfer instructions and is not a means of undertaking the payments themselves. The service can be used to transfer instructions for payments in a large number of currencies and is used in conjunction with transfer systems such as CHIPS. SWIFT is a widely used and internationally accepted transfer mechanism for payment instructions and other information. The set of currency codes used by the SWIFT system has become the international standard for currency recognition.

Overseas clearing systems

Clearing times vary around the world depending upon the banking system operating in a particular country. For example, in certain European countries one day's value is always lost to the bank in the clearing process, whereas in Australia clearing generally takes place on the same day that a cheque is paid into the bank. Some countries, such as the US and Italy, suffer delays because they do not have a nationwide clearing system. In general, however, the time taken for clearing depends upon the level of banking technology.

In an international transfer the funds will pass through more than one clearing system. This makes it all the more important that payment instructions are correctly given. This is illustrated in the following example.

A business wishes to make a deutschemark payment to a West German supplier. The business has a DM bank account held with the London branch of a German bank and the supplier has an account with the Frankfurt branch of a different German bank. The funds flows in the payment are shown in Figure 7.1.

Figure 7.1 *Funds flow for a transfer from the UK to West Germany*

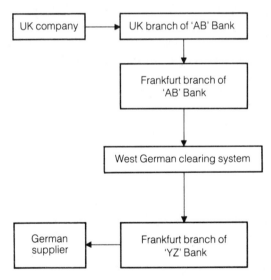

The correspondent banking system

International banks do not have branches in all financial centres where they wish to be represented. In order to maintain a presence in those countries where they do not have a branch, banks use a system of correspondent banks.

A correspondent bank acts as the representative of another bank in a particular country and processes all payments relating to that bank. When a transfer is made to a country where a bank has a correspondent rather than a branch, payment instructions should specify the correspondent bank.

Cash Transfers Within Overseas Countries

The transfer techniques vary within different banking systems. In some countries, such as Norway, the issue of cheques is rare and telegraphic transfers are used for almost all payments. In other areas, such as Latin America, telegraphic payment methods are uncommon and cheques are widely used, while other countries, such as Switzerland, make wide use of banker's drafts. The payment mechanisms used depend upon the level of technology and the regulatory environment within a particular country. In those countries which have restrictions placed upon the transfer of funds, documentary payment mechanisms are preferred as they are easier for the authorities to control.

8

Money Market Dealings

All businesses have a surplus or shortage of cash from time to time and need to deposit or borrow funds. Chapter 6 described how the use of deposit and overdraft accounts enables businesses to manage their cash position simply by holding accounts with their own bank branch. However, when businesses have a large amount of surplus funds or a sizeable borrowing requirement, they may get more favourable interest rates by dealing in the money market.

The London Money Market

The London 'money market' is where major banks and companies deal with their surplus or shortage positions. The money market is not a physical marketplace as such, merely the name given to the telephone trading which takes place in the City.

The money-market dealers in the City of London are generally located in the head offices of the major banks. These dealers make transactions with other international banks, brokers, bank branches and major corporate customers. They aim to make their profit from the margin between the borrowing and lending rates for sterling. The dealing day ends at 3pm in London and the dealers have strict limits on the amount of exposure (that is, sterling surplus or shortage) which they are allowed to hold by this time.

The money-market dealers take on both deposit and loan transactions from other parties, giving themselves a 'short' or 'long' sterling position. In order to regulate their own exposure, the dealers will deal with other banks in the money market. These deals are known as 'interbank' transactions, with the standard deal size normally being £5 million. Thus, the money-market dealers give better prices to corporate customers which wish to make transactions of this size, as these deals are easier to offset in the interbank market.

Interest calculations

Prices are always quoted as annual rates even though they are just referred to, for example, as 10.5 per cent. The interest is calculated according to the actual number of days elapsed on a 365–day basis. Thus, a deposit of £1 million placed on 15 June and maturing on 19 June at an interest rate of 10.5 per cent would earn interest of £1,150.68, calculated as follows:

$$1,000,000 \times \frac{10.5}{100} \times \frac{4}{365} = £1,150.68$$

This formula can be generalised as:

$$\text{Interest amount} = P \times \frac{i}{100} \times \frac{n}{365}$$

Where   p is the principal amount.
        i is the interest rate.
        n is the number of elapsed days.

Dealing on the money market is done on the basis of 'two-way prices', and a price for lending. The margin between these two prices is the bank's profit or 'turn'. The current market prices can be viewed via information services such as Reuters or Telerate where both the lending and borrowing prices will be displayed for a range of standard time periods. For example:

O/N	1 wk	2 wks	3 wks	1 mth	3 mths	6 mths	1 yr
10/10½	⅛/⅝	¼/¾	¼/¾	¼/⅞	⅜/11	11/11⅛	¼/½

Dealers inevitably use a great deal of shorthand and jargon in their work, largely because dealing has to be very fast, demanding a special coded language. An example can be seen in the above prices where the first column 'O/N' means overnight, that is, money deposited or borrowed from today until tomorrow. Sometimes prices are quoted as being 'T/N' or 'Tom-next' which means funds are deposited or borrowed from tomorrow to the next day.

The prices in this example are quoted in a shortened way since it is assumed that the customer understands the quoting procedures. The prices on the left-hand side are the interest rates which a bank would pay for deposits; the prices on the right are those which a bank would charge on loans. Prices are always quoted as traditional, rather than decimal fractions. The whole number of the interest rate (10 or 11 in the above example) is only quoted when it changes. In the above example 0.25/0.75 for a three-week period means that the bank would pay an interest rate of 10.25 per cent for deposits and charge 10.75 per cent for loans. Thus, the bank's margin would be 0.50 per cent.

The London market is at is busiest in the morning when prices are constantly changing. The prices which are quoted on Reuters and Telerate should only be taken as a guide to the market as they are likely to be out of date almost as soon as they appear on the screen. Generally the market prices move only fractionally up or down, but outside events, such as political announcements or the release of trade figures, can have a more dramatic and instant effect on prices. In addition, it is important to remember that the Bank of England is active in the London money markets, and each day there is an overall market shortage of surplus resulting from its actions.

Dealing Counterparties

A business wishing to deal on the London money markets can do so either through a bank branch, a broker or directly. The method depends upon the size of the borrowing or deposit, and the expertise of the business' staff who are conducting the deal.

Dealing through a bank branch

For valued customers, a bank branch will sometimes take deposits and lend money at more favourable rates than those which are available on bank deposits or overdrafts. These favourable rates are obtained by the bank branch dealing in the money markets through its own head-office money-market dealers. This money market dealing is 'invisible' to the customer who only takes the benefit of lower-cost borrowings or a higher return on deposits. The interest rates which the customer receives will be better than those available directly from the branch, but will be worse than the actual money market dealing rates. This is to allow for the bank's charge for providing this service.

Dealing through a broker

A business can normally obtain more favourable rates of interest for deposits by dealing through a money broker, rather than a bank branch. A money broker acts as a middleman between customers and the dealing rooms of major banks and is constantly aware of the latest market interest rates. Brokers quote their prices on a two-way basis, with the margin between the deposit and loan prices representing their profit margin.

Some businesses favour the use of brokers, even for large deals, on the grounds that the broker always knows where the best prices are being quoted. Other businesses prefer to build up their own relationships with the banking community and as a policy do not deal with brokers. However, the money broker does have a firm role in the market for smaller size deposits.

Brokers will also lend money, but in this case they are taking on the credit risk of the business concerned. As the brokers are in a middle role, they will only take on the credit risk of businesses when they are certain that they have a counterparty on which they can offset that risk.

Businesses which are regularly using their bank branch for deposits or loans of £250,000 or more should consider the use of money brokers. Before any dealing takes place, it is important to build up a rapport with the broker by making an introductory telephone call, preferably during the afternoon when the markets are not busy. If a business wishes to borrow money, the broker will have to be satisfied with the creditworthiness of the customer before any dealing takes place. Brokers are used to dealing with smaller clients and are generally helpful in guiding the inexperienced customer through the dealing process. However, since brokers are busy people it is important for a business to be professional when dealing with them.

Dealing with the money market dealers of banks

A business which has a requirement for large loan or deposit transactions may wish to deal directly with the money market dealers in major banks. Generally, it is not worthwhile for a business to deal directly in the money markets unless it has a regular requirement for transactions of £1 million or more. However, banks will often do occasional small transactions for good customers which regularly do large deals.

A business which wishes to embark upon money-market dealing will first need to decide which banks to approach. A good starting place for this is the head office of the business clearing bank. However, it is usually desirable to introduce an element of competition into the process by contracting more than one bank. The other banks may be approached on the basis of their size and standing in the market or through personal recommendation. It is important to bear in mind that sterling dealing is not confined to British banks and that some of the foreign banks which are represented in London offer very competitive prices for sterling deals.

The business should establish contact with the bank before any dealing takes place. This should be initiated by an introductory telephone call and possibly a meeting with the bank's dealers. Sometimes banks invite clients to visit their dealing rooms. This is worthwhile for the inexperienced dealer, providing a valuable insight into the frequently chaotic nature of the bank dealer's working environment.

The Dealing Process

Most banks' dealing rooms have 'corporate dealers' who are employed to speak to clients on the telephone and to arrange deals by getting rates and prices from the interbank dealers. These corporate dealers are employed to provide a service to clients by keeping them up to date with market developments, they are also used to dealing with relatively inexperienced client dealers. However, the fast pace of the money markets means that it is important for a client to be professional in its approach to dealing. This does not mean that client dealers need to be highly trained from the outset; merely that they must be cautious and level headed. A client dealer should consider the following points of advice.

1. Always be very clear in dealing. Once verbal agreement is reached, the client is committed to the deal, so it is essential that the details are understood by both parties. It is also important to remember that the bank views every money-market transaction as both a borrowing and a deposit. So, for example, if the client is depositing funds then the bank is simultaneously borrowing. A good discipline involves the client dealer repeating the details of the deal before the end of the telephone call to ensure that there are no misunderstandings,

2. Decide at the outset whether to tell the bank that the business is a potential depositor or borrower. Some businesses believe in asking the bank for a two-way price without disclosing which 'side' they are on. The rationale for this is that the bank may not give the most favourable price if it knows the client's position. Generally, businesses which have access to the current market prices, and which have built up a relationship with the bank, are better advised to tell the bank whether they wish to borrow or deposit. If the bank is particularly 'long' or 'short' of sterling, they may benefit if their position matches that of the bank,

3. Deal at good times. If possible, the client should avoid dealing during the lunch hour or just before 3pm. Preferably, the client should confine all its dealing to the morning when the market is busiest and the prices are strong. Overnight sterling rates can move dramatically in the afternoon as only a small amount of trading is done. Sometimes it is possible to borrow overnight funds very cheaply to refinance an overdraft, but dealing in the afternoon cannot be relied upon,

4. Deal in round amounts. The best interest rates will be obtained for large deals which the bank dealer can easily offset in the interbank market. If possible, deals for 'odd' amounts of pounds and pence should be avoided.

To illustrate the dealing process, the following is an example of a typical conversation which might take place between a client dealer and a bank dealer during the course of a transaction.

Example 6

Client Dealer	Bank Dealer
'Good Morning. This is the XYZ Company. What price are you quoting for overnight Sterling deposits?'	'I will take overnight Sterling at 10½ per cent.'
'In that case, I would like to deposit £2 million.'	'Agreed. I take £2 million overnight at 10½ per cent.'
'Where shall I pay the funds?'.	'Please pay the funds to my account number 12345678 at the City Bank in Broad Street.'
'On maturity, please pay back my principal, plus interest, to my account number 87654321 at the Town Bank in South Street.'	'Right. You deposit £2 million overnight at a rate of 10½ per cent. Thank you for the deal.'

Borrowing Funds

The two most popular ways for a business to borrow short-term funds in the money markets are through bank borrowings and acceptance credits.

Bank Borrowings

If the business wishes to borrow money from a bank it will be necessary for the bank's dealers to obtain approval for a line of credit to that company. This will involve the business providing the bank with sufficient accounting and other information for the bank to make an assessment of its creditworthiness. Once the bank is satisfied with the credit standing of the business, it will grant a loan facility and the business will be able to deal. This process can take several weeks, even if the business is successful in its application for a loan facility.

Loan facilities are granted on either a committed or uncommitted basis. The advantage of committed facilities is that the availability of funds is guaranteed whenever the business wishes to borrow money. However, the business has to pay a small margin for the facility, even when it is not a borrower. There is no charge for an uncommitted facility but the bank will not guarantee the availability of funds at all times.

Acceptance credits

In addition to borrowing directly from the banks, some businesses are able to borrow money by issuing acceptance bills. The issue of bills is arranged with a bank and takes place under a borrowing facility which has a specific acceptance option. The advantage of issuing bills is that interest rates tend to be slightly lower than for conventional borrowings. However, bills can only be issued for standard time periods, normally three or six months.

The interest on bills, as with many other documentary instruments, is paid on a discount basis. Thus, the client receives 'discounted proceeds' for the bills issued and repays the face value on maturity. For example, if £5 million three-month bills are issued at a discount rate of 10 ½ per cent, the client receives discounted proceeds of £4,869,109.59, calculated as follows.

$$5,000,000 - \left\{ (5,000,000 \times \frac{10.5}{100} \times \frac{91}{365}) \right\} = £5,000,000 - £130,890.41$$

$$= £4,869,109.59$$

This formula can be generalised as follows:

$$\text{Discounted proceeds} = P - \left\{ p \times \frac{i}{100} \times \frac{n}{365} \right\}$$

Where   p is the principal amount
i is the interest rate
n is the number of elapsed days

Bills can be traded between different parties in the money markets and, like some other documentary instruments, are said to be 'bearer' documents. This means that since no record is kept of the holders of the bills it is up to the holders to collect their proceeds on the maturity date. Bearer instruments are valuable documents which must be stored under secure conditions.

The normal process for a business issuing bills is as follows.

1. A loan facility with an acceptance bill option is agreed with the bank.
2. A supply of bank bills is sent to the client by the bank.
3. Before an issue, the client completes the bills by filling in the required sterling amounts and has the bills endorsed by authorised signatories.
4. The bills are sent by secure courier to the bank.
5. Upon instructions from the client the bank issues (sells) the bills to other banks and financial institutions.
6. The client receives the discounted proceeds of the issue.
7. On maturity the client repays the face value amount to the bank which in turn repays the bill holders.

Under Bank of England regulations, bills must only be issued up to the amount of the 'authorised' trade which the business has outstanding. Broadly speaking, authorised trade is the import of raw materials or the export of finished goods, but any business wishing to issue bills should ask its bank for a full description of authorised trade. The trade against which the bill is issued must be stated on the face of the bill. This is known as 'clausing'.

Investing Funds

The two most popular means for a business to invest short-term funds in London are bank deposits and the purchase of Certificates of Deposit.

Bank deposits

The dealing process for bank deposits is similar to the process for borrowing funds. However, by taking deposits the bank is not exposed to any credit risk and there is no need for a facility to be established. It is worth remembering that the business is exposed to the credit risk of the bank and should therefore exercise some caution when placing funds. The business must establish a list of exposure limits to all banks with which it intends to deal. This list, and any changes to it, should preferably be agreed at board level within the company. All deals should then be recorded on the list against the relevant bank and deposits should not be made which will breach the agreed limits. Businesses do not normally disclose to banks any details of their limits list.

Investing in Certificates of Deposit

Certificates of Deposit (CDs) are tradeable loan instruments issued by the banks. A business can invest in a CD as an alternative to placing a deposit with a bank. The interest on CD always tends to be slightly lower than that which is payable on deposits, but CDs are a liquid investment which the business can sell if a sudden cash shortage arises.

CDs can be purchased from the banks and discount houses on the London money market and, like acceptance bills, are quoted on the basis of a discount rate. Thus, the business invests the discounted value of the CD and, if it holds the CD to maturity, receives the full face value from the issuer. CDs which are not held to maturity can be sold at a discount rate which is dictated by the market, and which depends upon the yield of the CD compared to the current market interest rates for the same period.

It is important to remember that the credit risk with a CD lies with the issuer and not with the bank that is selling the instrument. The exposure should be recorded in the business' exposure records against the limit for the issuing bank. Thus, a business which is purchasing CDs should always enquire into the name of the issuer before agreeing to deal.

Interest Rate Exposure

Businesses which invest or borrow money at floating rates of interest are exposed to adverse market movements in interest rates. Thus, businesses which are depositing funds will lose interest income if interest rates fall, and businesses which are borrowing funds will have to pay higher interest charges if interest rates rise.

The only way for a business to avoid the adverse effects of interest-rate movements is to enter into hedging contracts to protect the interest rate from market movements. The two most popular interest-rate hedging techniques are interest rate options and Future Rate Agreements (FRAs).

Interest-rate options

Interest-rate options can be purchased from banks. They are contracts which give the holder the right to make a deposit or loan for a specified interest rate on a specified date in the future. As the name implies, an option gives the right to make a specified transaction, but there is no obligation to do so.

The use of an interest-rate option is best illustrated by the following example. A company anticipates a receipt of £1 million in two months' time. Interest rates are currently 10 per cent but the company expects them to fall. The company purchases an option to make a £1 million deposit at 10 per cent in two months' time. The company pays a fee to the bank for this option. If after two months, interest rates have fallen to 9 per cent the company will exercise the option and deposit funds at 10 per cent. However, if interest rates have unexpectedly risen to 11 per cent, then the company will allow the option to expire and will deposit the funds in the market at the higher interest rate.

Future Rate Agreements (FRAs)

FRAs are similar to options in that the business contracts to take a loan or deposit for a future period at an agreed interest rate. However, with an FRA the contract exists irrespective of the movement in interest rates and a compensating payment is made between the business and the bank at the start of the deposit or loan period. If an FRA had been used in the above example, the outcome would have been as follows:

The company purchases an FRA to deposit £1 million at 10 per cent in two month's time. If market rates are 9 per cent after two months, then the bank would pay the company a sum equivalent to 1 per cent of £1 million for the deposit period, discounted back to the beginning of the period. If market rates are 11 per cent after two months, then the company would pay the bank the same amount.

The difference between an FRA and an option is that an FRA fixes the interest regardless of market movements, whereas an option allows the customer to benefit from advantageous movements in interest rates.

Deal Documentation

When a deal is agreed between a business and a bank it has to be confirmed in writing by both parties. At the time of dealing it is normal for both the client dealer and the bank dealer to complete a deal slip which records the details of the deal. An example deal slip is shown in Example 7. The client's deal slip is then used to update the manual or computer records of the client's position. The details from the deal slip are used to produce a confirmation letter which is signed by the authorised signatories of the client and mailed to the bank. An example of a confirmation letter is shown in Example 9.

The bank also mails a written confirmation to the client which should be matched to the copy of the company's confirmation letter. The matching of confirmations is an important control over the dealing process as it identifies discrepancies between the records of the client and the bank.

The deal slip is also used to generate a confirmation letter to the bank which holds the client's current account in cases when a payment has to be made out of the current account to meet the obligations of the deal. This occurs, for example, when funds are put on deposit or when loans are repaid. An example confirmation letter to the account holding bank is shown in Example 9.

A flow chart showing the flow of deal documentation and information is shown in Figure 8.1.

Dealing Controls

Money-market deals are agreed over the telephone with both parties being committed to the contract once a verbal agreement is reached. It is important that the dealing process is adequately controlled to prevent accidental or fraudulent activities resulting in losses for the business. There are primary risks involved which controls should seek to eliminate.

1. Funds being transferred out of one of the business' bank accounts and misdirected to an unauthorised account. This can occur when payment instructions for legitimate payments are incorrectly given to the bank and underlines the need for accurate payment instructions.

2. Funds which are due to the business not being received in the designated bank account at the correct time. Once again, funds can be misdirected if incorrect or incomplete payment instructions are given.

3. Transactions not being properly recorded, resulting in 'hidden' exposures to interest-rate movements and incorrect cash-flow data.

4. Unnecessary payments being made out of the business bank accounts. This leads to a loss of interest whilst the funds are retrieved and the company incurs the unnecessary charge for the transfer.

The process of telephone dealing, giving settlement instructions and producing the written confirmation should be carried out by three different individuals. Such a control requirement will present practical difficulties for smaller businesses which have only limited resources. However, an acceptable level of control can be implemented where two or more individuals are involved with cash management. For *a one-person cash management team*, controls *are clearly more problematic* and there may be inherent control weaknesses in such a small operation, particularly resulting from lack of effective cover when the person is absent.

Example 7 *Deal slip*

Loan deposit
Amount (£)_____
Bank_____
From (Date)_____
To (Date)_____
Interest Rate % per annum_____
Bank Dealer_____
Company Dealer_____
Settlement Instructions_____

Example 8 *Confirmation letter*

To: The Manager
XYZ Bank plc
21 Broad Street
London   3 August 198X

Dear Sir,

Re: Confirmation of £2,000,000 loan

This is to confirm that you have loaned us £2,000,000 from 2 August 198X to 2 September 198X at an interest rate of 10.5 per cent per annum.

Please pay the funds to our account number 12345678 with the South Bank plc, City Street Branch. On maturity, we will repay the loan plus accrued interest to your account number 24681357 with the ABC Bank plc, South Road Branch.

Yours faithfully,

Authorised signatory   Authorised signatory

Example 9 *Confirmation letter to the account holding bank*

To: Manager
South Bank plc
City Street Branch
London   1 September

Dear Sir,

Re: Account number 12345678

This is to confirm our telephone request to yourselves to pay the sum of £2,017,835.62 to the ABC Bank plc, South Road Branch, and to credit the account number 24681357 held in the name of the XYZ Bank plc for value 2 September 198X.

Yours faithfully,

Authorised signatory   Authorised signatory

Figure 8.1   *The flow of deal documentation and information*

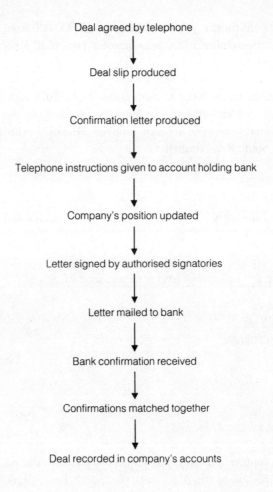

Deal agreed by telephone

↓

Deal slip produced

↓

Confirmation letter produced

↓

Telephone instructions given to account holding bank

↓

Company's position updated

↓

Letter signed by authorised signatories

↓

Letter mailed to bank

↓

Bank confirmation received

↓

Confirmations matched together

↓

Deal recorded in company's accounts

9

Foreign Exchange

The UK is a trading nation with many businesses being involved in overseas trade, whether as importers of raw materials or as exporters of finished goods. In addition to their normal business, these companies are involved in foreign currency transactions and the management of exchange-rate risk.

Foreign Currency Dealing

The previous chapter considered how a business can use the sterling money markets to borrow or deposit funds at favourable rates of interest. However, many businesses need to deal in foreign currencies as well as sterling.

London is one of the largest foreign exchange markets in the world where all the freely exchanged currencies can be traded. The foreign-exchange market is a telephone market which includes all the major international banks. Many of the principles of dealing apply equally to money market and foreign currency transactions. Consequently, this chapter will not cover the documentation and control of dealing since it was included in the previous one.

Foreign Exchange Contracts

A foreign exchange contract takes place when one currency is bought for another currency at a specified exchange rate and for a specified date. The two types of foreign exchange contract which are most commonly used for dealing are the spot contract and the forward contract.

Spot dealing

Deals which are done for 'spot' value are effective two working days ahead of the deal date. For example, a deal done on Thursday would be effective on Monday. Although the contract would be made on Thursday, the funds would be transferred on Monday.

Forward dealing

Forward deals are those done for future dates beyond the 'spot' date. The forward markets for most of the major traded currencies stretch further than one year ahead, meaning that deals can be agreed for dates more than one year into the future.

There are two types of forward-foreign exchange transaction: the outright forward and the forward option. An outright forward contract is one which is agreed for some specified future date. A forward option contract is one which matures within a specified future time period, rather than one particular date. This gives flexibility when the exact timing of future currency flows are uncertain. It is important to note that forward option contracts are only forward contracts with some flexibility of the maturity date. They should not be confused with currency-option contracts which are dealt with later in this chapter.

Exchange rates

In the London market most major currencies are quoted against sterling so that a sterling/US dollar rate of 1.4500 means that for every £1 the trader would receive US$1.45. Internationally, most currencies are quoted against the US dollar. Thus, a US dollar/deutschemark rate of 1.8000 means that for every US$1 the trader would receive DMK1.80.

Foreign currency rates, like money market rates, are quoted as two-way prices with a 'spread' or margin between the prices which represents the bank's profit. Thus, the exchange rate for sterling against the deutschemark might be quoted as 2.8080/2.8090.

The left-hand side of the quote is known as the 'bid' rate and the right-hand side is known as the 'offer' rate. Thus, the offer rate minus the bid rate will equal the bank's spread. In reality, quotes are rarely shown in such detail as the one above. This exchange rate is likely to be shown as 2.8080/90, and may be verbally quoted as '80/90'. Dealers assume that the customer knows the main part of the rate (or 'big figure') is 2.80.

The bid rate is the rate at which the bank will buy deutschemarks for sterling, and the offer rate is the rate at which the bank will sell deutschemarks for sterling.

The derivation of forward exchange rates

Foreign exchange rates can be viewed via Reuters or Telerate where they are shown as follows:

	Spot	1 wk	2 wks	1 mth	3 mths
£/US$	1.4000/10	50/40	55/45	55/45	80/60

The first column shows the spot rate and the subsequent columns are for deals done for forward-value dates. It is important to notice that the numbers shown in the forward columns do not represent exchange rates as such, but represent 'swap points'. These are the figures which adjust the spot rate into future rates. Swap points may represent either a 'premium' or a 'discount' to the spot rate. The swap points are said to be premium points when the right-hand number is lower than the left-hand one. Swap points are said to be at a discount when the right-hand number is greater than the left-hand number. In order to calculate the outright forward rate from the spot rate and swap points, it is necessary to add discount points or subtract premium points. This sounds complicated, but the rule is:

Rising points ⟶   discount ⟶ add
Falling points ⟶   premium ⟶ subtract

To calculate the outright two-week forward rate from the

above example, the calculation will be:

	Bid	Offer
Spot rate	1.4000	1.4010
Premium points	− 0.0055	− 0.0045
Outright rate	1.3945	1.3965

The outright two-week forward rate is 1.3945/65 which gives a spread of 0.0020 (known as '20 pips') whereas the spread on the spot rate was 0.0010 ('10 pips'). Thus, the spread widens as the time period increases. This is not, as many people suppose, to reward the dealers for the greater risk of forward transactions. The forward rates are derived from the spot rate and the interest differentials between the two currencies, and the widening spread in this case reflects the difference between sterling and dollar interest rates.

Assume that the £/US$ spot rate is 1.5500, sterling three-month interest rates are 10 per cent per annum and dollar three-month interest rates are 8 per cent per annum. The following example shows how the forward-exchange rate is derived from these present day figures.

A company has £1,000 which is to be translated into US dollars in three month's time. The foreign exchange market for the major currencies is a perfect market so the company should be in the same position if it either invests the sterling and makes the exchange in three months' time, or makes the exchange now and invests the dollars for three months. This is illustrated below.

Table 9.1

	Invest £; Exchange later	Exchange now; Invest $
Starting point	£1,000	£1,000 = $1,550
Interest rate	10%	8%
Interest after 3 months	£25	$31
Proceeds in 3 months	£1,025	$1,581

Since the two options must give the same end value (otherwise trading would soon bring the market back to equilibrium), the three-month forward exchange rate can be derived from the ratio of the two amounts of proceeds.

Thus, the three-month forward rate is:

$$\frac{1,581}{1,025} = 1.5424$$

Since this is a lower number than the spot rate, the points would be subtracted to calculate the forward rate from the spot rate. This implies that, in this case, the forward rate stands at a premium to the spot rate.

Foreign Exchange Exposure

A business is exposed to the effects of foreign exchange rates if adverse movements in the rates can cause lower losses or a lowering of income. This is illustrated in the following examples.

1. A UK company purchases the raw materials for its products from West Germany and pays for them in deutschemarks. The finished goods are sold in the UK for sterling. This company suffers from foreign exchange exposure as any strengthening in the value of the deutschemark against sterling will result in increased raw-material costs, while it may not be possible for the company to increase the price of finished goods.
2. A UK company has a US subsidiary which pays a quarterly US dollar dividend to the parent company. This company also suffers from foreign-exchange exposure as any weakening in the value of the US dollar relative to sterling will diminish the value of these dividends.
3. Company X, a UK company, buys the raw materials for its products in the UK and sells the finished goods in the UK. The only competitor in the market, company Y, buys raw materials in Japan and sells the finished goods in the UK. Although

company X is a wholly domestic producer, it is still affected by movements in foreign-exchange rates because a weakening in the value of the yen against sterling could enable company Y to lower its prices and increase market share.

Currency Hedging

Currency hedging instruments are available from banks and financial institutions, enabling the business to avoid the adverse effects of exchange rate movements. The principle behind currency hedging is that the bank takes on the risk of the exchange rate movement from the business. The most widely used currency hedging techniques are forward contracts and currency options.

Forward contracts as hedging instruments

Forward contracts fix the future exchange rate and hedge the value of currency flows. For example, a company which has to pay two million US dollars to a supplier in two months' time can make the exchange now at a rate of 1.6000 with a value date two months ahead. This gives the company certainty regarding the cost of the payment. If the US dollar has strengthened to 1.5000 in two month's time then the company has saved £83,333, calculated as follows.

Purchase of US$2,000,000 1.6000 = cost of £1,250,000
Purchase of US$2,000,000 1.5000 = cost of £1,333,333

$$£1,333,333 - £1,250,000 = £83,333$$

The above example illustrates the fact that with a forward contract there is no potential to benefit from favourable movements in the exchange rate after the contract has been agreed. However, as no fees are payable for forward contracts, they are a low-cost means of hedging currency flows.

Currency options

Currency options allow the business to benefit from favourable movements in exchange rates after the hedge has been agreed. However, a front-end fee is payable for a currency option which sometimes makes this hedging technique seem unacceptably expensive.

Currency options can be purchased from banks and give the business the right (but not the obligation) to make a currency transaction at a specified exchange rate at a specified future time. The benefits of currency options can be illustrated by further use of the above example.

In the first case, where the exchange rate moved to 1.5000, the company would have been worse off if it had purchased a currency option at 1.6000 instead of making the forward transaction. This is because the proceeds would be the same for each transaction, but the company would have paid a fee for the currency option.

In the second case, where the exchange rate moved to 1.7000, the company would have been better off if it had purchased a currency option at 1.6000 instead of making the forward transaction. This is because the company could let the option expire and make the currency exchange at the prevailing spot rate (1.7000). In this case the company would have sacrificed the option fee but would have benefited from the favourable movement in exchange rates.

A great deal of jargon is attached to the use of currency options, but the above description covers their essential features. A business which is considering the use of currency options should find an experienced bank which will devote the resources to helping the customer understand this complex instrument.

10
Exporting

Businesses which seek to increase sales by exporting face many risks and requirements which do not apply to equivalent sales to UK customers. The commercial risks which apply in the home market are now increased by political risks (revolutions, wars or government policy changes) and exchange-rate risks (some countries in Latin America and Africa, for example, occasionally impose payment restrictions due to shortage of foreign currency).

Creditworthiness of Customers

Before giving credit to export customers an assessment should be made to ascertain the risk of non-payment. The sources of information and techniques which can be used to judge the creditworthiness of a prospective customer include those applicable to the home market which were covered in Chapter 1:

- Bank reference.
- Two trade references.
- Credit-reporting agencies.
- Visits (usually only justified in the case of large customers).
- Analysis of company accounts (availability, quantity and quality of information varies widely from country to country).

Sources of information particular to export markets include:

- Local agents, particularly in developing countries are often the only person who has direct contact with the customer.

This makes their assessments of credit-worthiness important.

● Export Credit Guarantee Department (ECGD) will carry out credit-worthiness checks on both customers and countries.

● British Overseas Trade Board (BOTB), which is a UK government agency. It provides information and assistance either free of charge or at minimal cost on many aspects of overseas markets including credit ratings of importers. This service if of more use when assessing customers in developing countries.

When assessing the creditworthiness of export customers it is advisable for a business to obtain as much information as possible. It should use a combination of as many of the above sources as is practical.

Credit Limits

These should be set for export customers, using the same principles as for UK customers. When setting the limit a business should consider the effect of the time it takes to ship goods, which can be several weeks. Also, delays can occur in the movement of funds back to the UK. These factors may indicate the need for a higher credit limit than would be normal in the UK as the limit may have to cover an extra four to six-week credit period.

Terms of Payment

The terms of payment for export customers are complicated by the terms of contract and the documentation which apply to export trade.

Terms of contract

The terms relating to the shipping of goods to export customers determine when the goods and risk pass to the customer, who also pays for freight and insurance. The principal terms are:

Ex-works. The customer arranges for collection from the supplier's premises and pays the freight and insurance costs. The goods and risk pass to the customer when he is notified the goods are at his disposal.

Free on Board. FOB terms require the supplier to place the goods on board a ship or aircraft specified by the customer and to pay for all expenses up to that point. The customer arranges and pays for freight and insurance. Unless otherwise specified the goods and risk pass to the customer when they are loaded onto the ship or aircraft.

Cost, insurance and freight. CIF terms relate to the sale of the documents relating to the goods. The supplier arranges and pays for freight and insurance to the port or airport specified by the customer.

Cost and freight. C&F terms as above, but the customer arranges and pays for insurance.

Documentation. Export documentation is particularly important as payment delays are often the result of documentation errors. The principal documents are:

- *Invoice.* As well as the information found in a normal invoice the authorities in the importing country may require the terms of contract (eg FOB), currency of invoice and declaration of the origin of the goods.
- *Insurance certificate.* For terms where the supplier is responsible for insurance a certificate is required by the customer or his agents.
- *Bills of lading.* These are very important documents as they are a receipt for the goods given by the shipping company and also documents of title. Bills are normally raised in sets of three original copies. Any one of these, on presentation, can

give title to the goods.
- *Airway bills*. Are receipts only and are not documents of title.
- *Certificate of origin*. The authorities in the importing country often require a declaration stating the origin of the goods. This is normally evidenced by a certificate authenticated by a Chamber of Commerce.

Terms of payment

The shortest possible payment terms should be negotiated with overseas customers. Ideally the payment should be in sterling or in a currency which is not subject to exchange limitations. The five usual methods of payment are:

- *In advance*. This is the most secure method for exporters, but is unacceptable to the majority of customers. Also, some countries have exchange-control regulations which do not permit this.
- *Upon receipt*. This method allows the customer to inspect the goods before payment. This is best if the two parties have an established trading relationship and payments are not subject to exchange control.
- *By collection*. This is through a bank (or forwarding agent) in the customer's country. An invoice, a bill of exchange and any customs and exchange clearance documents are sent with instructions to the customer's bank. The goods are consigned either to the customer or to the bank. The bank confirms receipt of goods, arranges collection of monies due and releases the bill of exchange. This is suitable for countries where this procedure is well established but payment can be delayed due to documentation and remittance difficulties.
- *By documentary letter of credit*. Payment is made by the customer or customer's bank to the supplier's bank. This guarantees payment and overcomes exchange difficulties. The supplier's bank does not release payment to the supplier until the conditions specified in the letter of credit are satisfied. A documentary credit is usually 'irrevocable', that is, the obligations of all parties cannot be revoked without the

agreement of all concerned. The payment may be 'at sight', that is, on presentation of specified documents or 'upon acceptance' at some fixed future date.

- *Open-account terms* are similar to those operating in the UK market for credit customers. These are normally used where the customer is well-established in a country free from political and exchange risks. The methods of paying an open account include cheques, bankers drafts, mail transfers and telegraphic transfers.

Collection of Amounts Due

The methods of pursuing overdue accounts in the UK are largely applicable to overseas customer accounts. Additional complications are introduced due to language, public holiday and time differences. Where a local agent acts for the supplier he should not receive his commission until the payment is received for the goods.

Many UK-based collection agencies have overseas branches and offer the service of overseas debt collection. The quality of service varies and the fee for collection can be considerable (up to 25 per cent of the debt is common). As with UK customers, the instigation of legal proceedings to collect overseas customer debts should be a last resort. Such action is likely to be very expensive and could take many months to complete.

Finance For Exports

Credit terms given to overseas customers are generally longer than those for customers in the UK. The supplier has to finance the extended credit period, otherwise he may find he has become insolvent even though he has increased sales through exporting.

Export Credits Guarantee Department (ECGD)

All industrialised western countries offer some form of government insurance and finance to their exports. The British Government provides a very sophisticated service through the ECGD.

The ECGD's insurance policies are designed to provide protection against major export risks. The cover provided is typically 90 per cent of buyer risks (the risk associated with a particular customer) and between 90–95 per cent of market risks (the risk associated with a particular country or region). If a claim for non-payment is made and met by ECGD, the exporter remains responsible for collection of the debt. Such insurance policies are generally accepted as suitable collateral security for obtaining bank finance. The services provided by ECGD include the following.

Comprehensive cover for continuous repetitive business. This offers protection against both commercial and political risk. Exporters are required to offer the whole of their export business so as to diversify the risk as much as possible. Exporters pay an annual premium supplemented by monthly premiums which vary according to the level of export sales.

Guarantees for supplier credit finance. The holder of comprehensive cover may use his policy to borrow from banks at a preferential rate of 0.625 per cent over bank base rate. The cost of this service is approximately 0.25 per cent per annum.

Specific cover for individual export contracts. This is designed for particularly large contracts on credit terms of two years or more. Cover and premiums are negotiated individually. With the protection of this security the banks provide finance at preferential interest rates which are determined according to the buyer's country and the length of credit terms.

Guarantees for buyer's credit finance. These enable importers of UK capital goods to obtain loans from UK banks to finance such purchases. The exporter normally receives 15 or 20 per cent of the contract price direct from the buyer. The remainder is paid to the exporter from a loan made to the buyer. This loan is guaranteed by ECGD. A minimum contract value of £1 million is normally required for such guarantees.

Supplementary services. These include assistance with collection of foreign debts, credit-worthiness checks on imports and countries, and specialised cover for exchange-rate fluctuation, overseas investments, cost escalation, performance bonds and insolvency of project partners.

Export houses

A business entering an export market should consider using the services of export houses as they can help solve many problems through the use of their financial strength and expertise. Export houses provide finance for exporters and include:

- Export merchants who act as principals on their own account.
- Export agents who represent the exporter.
- Confirming houses who deal on behalf of the buyer.

11

Capital Structure

The relationship between permanent or long-term capital and working capital depends upon the type of business. Many manufacturing businesses require a significant investment in fixed assets such as machinery and equipment with a relatively smaller investment in working capital. In contrast, retail businesses require a larger proportion of working capital, particularly in the form of stock.

Whatever the business the amount of permanent capital required will be determined by the amount of credit both allowed and received. Many of the large retail businesses have been able to finance their rapid expansion through the credit given by their suppliers. As they largely sell their goods for cash while receiving 30–days credit from their suppliers they have reduced their requirement for longer-term capital.

A business' capital structure will be made up of a combination of the following forms of finance:

- ordinary share capital
- redeemable ordinary shares
- reserves
- preference shares
- debentures
- long-term loans
- current liabilities

Financing Policy

When deciding upon a suitable capital structure a business has many factors to consider. Most businesses have varying requirements for capital depending upon their stage of growth, and it is usual to find businesses with suboptimum structures which have evolved over time. The following factors are important when deciding upon the most appropriate capital structure:

1. Purpose. The type of finance can often be related to the purpose for which the finance will be used. For example, an increase in sales will require an additional investment in working capital, but the increased sales should eventually finance the required working capital itself. It is common to match the acquisition of fixed assets, such as land and buildings, with long-term sources of finance, such as ordinary share capital or debentures. Machines such as a lathe may be financed by a five-year loan or it may be leased.

2. Amount of capital required. Creditors will only finance a business up to a certain limit. Most businesses (other than retailers) regard a proportion of their working capital requirements as being fixed as they constantly have to finance part of their stock and debtors. This element is normally financed from longer-term sources.

3. Industry norm. A business is unlikely to adopt a capital structure significantly different from the norm of the industry in which it trades. The capital markets tend to make it difficult and expensive for a business to stray from the norm and more expensive capital weakens the business' competitiveness.

4. Risk. Each form of financing carries a different risk and a business attitude towards risk will influence its choice of capital structure. Raising long-term finance carries with it the risk that it is only actually required for a short period. One example of this is where increased stocks and debtors were thought to be necessary due to an upturn in trading conditions which turned out to be a change in buying pattern. The risk involved in raising short-term finance is mainly the possibility that it may not be renewed by the lender when the agreed term has elapsed. The need for the capital may, however, remain.

The suppliers of funds will perceive a different kind of risk from the business. They will only provide funds, long or short-term, debt or equity, if the risk of an adequate return and repayment is acceptable. The security offered in terms of tangible assets is a relevant factor in determining risk.

5. Cost. The after-tax cost of each type of financing will affect the capital structure chosen. This can vary depending upon the business' circumstances, environment and type and source of finance.

6. Existing capital structure. If a business has a large amount of debt within its existing structure it may find it difficult to finance further asset acquisitions through raising long-term debt. This factor is related to risk perception, discussed above.

7. Profitability. The profit earning capacity, size and variability, in relation to capital employed, determines, (to an extent) the types of finance available to a business. Providers of capital will consider past profit record as well as future prospects.

8. Environment. The external environment in which a business exists is influenced by a number of factors which are in a state of constant flux. Political, social, technological and economic factors affect a business financial structure directly and indirectly. A direct influence may be exerted through the fortunes of the industry, and indirectly the state of capital markets, depressed or otherwise, affects the availability of finance.

Gearing

The above factors impinge on the decision as to which capital structure a business should adopt. The final choice of structure invariably includes a mixture of debt and equity finance. Long-term debt, in the context of gearing, commonly includes bank overdrafts and short-term bank loans. This is because overdrafts (although strictly repayable on demand) are normally in existence for long periods, and short-term loans are also renewed or 'rolled over'.

The gearing ratio is commonly used to determine whether a business has a capital structure which is highly geared:

Gearing ratio =
$$\frac{\text{Long-term debt} + \text{preference shares}}{\text{Ordinary shareholders funds.}}$$

A highly-geared business is one with a high proportion of prior charge capital. Some investors consider a ratio of 1:1 to be the 'rule of thumb' for this ratio, implying that assets could decline in value by up to 50 per cent before threatening the security of the funds provided from their loans.

If the gearing ratio is 2:1 the claims of the providers of debt and short-term credit are not so safe; assets need to fall in value by only 33 per cent before their claims are threatened.

As with all ratios the gearing ratio should be used with care, as accounting policies and the point in time that it was produced can cause severe distortions. It is more meaningful to compare the ratios for a business over a period of time and to compare the ratio of a business with the norm for the industry, this assisting in answering whether the gearing is unduly high or low.

Investors in a business often consider the risk involved with a particular capital structure in terms of the interest cover:

Interest cover =
$$\frac{\text{Profit before interest and tax}}{\text{Interest}}$$

This ratio shows the number of times the interest payable is covered by earnings. The amount of cover required by lenders varies according to their attitude towards risk and economic conditions generally. As a rule of thumb, the provider of unsecured debt finance would require cover of about five times.

Debt versus equity

Trading conditions vary from time-to-time and cause the choice of capital structure to significantly affect a business' profitability and liquidity, and therefore its survival. The simplified examples below illustrate the effect of differing capital structures under varying trading conditions.

Table 11.1

	Structure 'A' £	Structure 'B' £
Ordinary shares	100,000	75,000
Long-term loans	50,000	75,000
Earnings (before interest and tax)	50,000	50,000
Interest (at 15%)	7,500	11,250
Tax at 35%	14,875	13,560
% return on ordinary shares	27.6	33.6
Gearing ratio	0.5:1	1:1

Table 11.2

	Structure 'A' £	Structure 'B' £
Earnings	10,000	10,000
% return ordinary shares	1.6	−1.1*

*Assumes tax loss carried forward.

Structure 'A', which is lower geared than Structure 'B', gives shareholders a poorer return when trading conditions are favourable. Under such conditions Structure 'B' gives a return of 33.6 per cent against 27.6 per cent for Structure 'A'. The higher the gearing under these conditions the higher the return for shareholders.

If conditions changed to those in example 2 where earnings have fallen to £10,000, the return for ordinary shareholders falls to 1.6 per cent under Structure 'A'. Under Structure 'B' the shareholders receive a negative return, that is, they do not receive any return and must also finance the shortfall in interest payments to lenders. It is under such conditions that highly-geared businesses are vulnerable to liquidation.

Half the new business ventures fail within the first three years. This alarming statistic has relevance to the decision of the levels of debt a business should include in its capital structure, as the most cited reason for the failure of new ventures is the lack of capital and badly-managed debt. Badly-managed debt or too high a gearing level should be avoided as the lure of extra profits can lead to the business' downfall. A balanced capital structure is essential for long-term survival.

Sources of Finance

Short-term sources of finance such as trade credit, invoice discounting and factoring have been covered in detail in Chapter 1. Other sources of short-term debt finance include bank overdrafts and loans, which for many businesses are a permanent feature of their capital structure. They are effectively a form of long-term finance. Other sources of long-term finance are equity finance, hire purchase, leasing arrangements, retained earnings, and financial assistance from the government.

Debt finance

Debt finance consists of bank overdrafts, loan capital and debentures.

Bank overdrafts. These are the most flexible source of finance because they can be arranged or varied at short notice. They are mainly available from clearing banks, but merchant banks also provide overdraft facilities. Strictly speaking, overdrafts are repayable on demand but it is common for a business to have a sizeable overdraft facility available and used indefinitely. In the case of smaller businesses it is common for banks to require security for overdraft facilities either in the form of collateral or personal guarantees from directors.

Loan capital. This is provided by many institutions and the term of the loan may vary from a few months up to 20 years or more. Interest charges vary depending upon source, risk and period involved, and may be either a fixed percentage or variable (linked to base lending rates or the London Interbank Offered Rate, LIBOR). Repayments may be monthly, yearly, or some other fixed period; it is quite common for no repayments to be made in the early part of the life of the loan.

Loans may be secured or unsecured. As with overdrafts, lenders may insist on having some control over the affairs of the borrower's business and could require regular information on such aspects of the business as cashflow, profitability and future plans.

The list below indicates some of the sources of loan capital:

- Clearing banks.
- Merchant banks.
- Finance houses.
- Investors In Industry (3i's).
- Syndicates (usually a number of banks).
- Pension funds.
- Insurance companies.

Debentures. These are a form of debt finance secured on the specific assets of a business by means of either a fixed or floating charge. As the providers of such finance (often pension funds) have substantial security they regard this type of investment as virtually risk-free. The business, however, has some risk, in that interest on the debt has to to be paid whether or not the business is trading profitably. It is often debenture holders who petition for the winding-up of companies as they would be the first to receive all, or part of their investment.

Equity finance

Equity finance is raised by offering investors a stake in a company through the purchase of ordinary shares. The company may be 'private', in which case shares will not be traded on a recognised stock exchange, or it may be 'public', in which case its shares will be traded.

Companies can raise equity finance from institutions and private investors through either public or private sources. Public sources include a *full Stock Exchange listing*, where the company is required to have an established trading record with a minimum of five years unqualified accounts. Costs of 'going public' are normally in excess of £300,000 and small to medium-size companies should normally only consider this source of finance where the requirement for finance is large and long-term.

Funds may be raised through a company's quotation on the *Unlisted Securities Market* (USM). As with a full Stock Exchange listing the company has certain requirements to fulfil, including providing significant amounts of information. The costs of achieving a quotation can be substantial, in the order of £150,000, but the company will find the raising of equity finance easier than if no quotation existed.

The *Third Market* was established in 1987 by the Stock Exchange to provide a public market for new or smaller businesses which do not have the three-year track record required by the USM. The likely candidates for the Third Market are companies in need of an equity injection, but which are too small for the USM.

The Over-the-Counter (OTC) market for shares does not require a specific track record for a business. Entry to the OTC markets can be made either through placings by a market maker, with its clients at a fixed price (in some cases underwritten by institutions), or by offers for sale.

Private sources of equity finance include institutions who provide *venture or development capital*. These institutions include clearing banks and their subsidiaries, Investors In Industry (3i's), finance houses, pension funds and insurance companies. A further source of finance is through a *private placing* whereby shares are bought by an institution through an arrangement which is normally negotiated though an intermediary such as a merchant bank.

Other sources of finance

Hire purchase is a source of finance particularly used to buy fixed assets such as cars and machinery. This can be an expensive form of finance and is provided by finance houses and 3i's.

Leasing has been a very popular form of finance in recent years. Up to 31 March 1986 it provided a particularly competitive source of finance for business which, because of tax losses or for other reasons, were unable to take advantage of the available first-year capital allowances. With the ending of first-year allowances for most equipment from 1 April 1986, and their replacement by 25 per cent writing-down allowances, the tax advantage of leasing is greatly reduced. Leasing can still be an advantageous form of finance, but the decision between leasing an asset or obtaining a loan to finance its purchase is less clear, and individual circumstances must be considered carefully.

A variation on the leasing theme is *sale and leaseback* whereby a business sells an asset, usually land and buildings, to an institution and then leases the asset over a specific period.

Retained Earnings

The largest source of finance for businesses in the UK to date has been internally generated funds. These consist of profits after tax plus depreciation (a non-cashflow item) less dividends paid. Traditionally businesses have used the 'ploughed back' profits to finance growth through fixed-asset acquisitions, funding working capital and investment in research and development. Retained earnings are dependent upon the dividend policy adopted by the business which could involve the distribution of all, none or a proportion of its current and past profit, after tax, to the shareholders.

In an ideal world a business would only retain profits within the business if it could earn a higher rate of return on those funds than was available elsewhere. If highly-profitable projects existed within the business, the shareholder would get a return on his investment through the appreciation in the value of his shares (capital gain), rather than through receipt of a dividend. Reality tends to be different from the theory and dividend policy is influenced by many factors.

Dividend policy has an effect on a company's share price and investors can and do behave irrationally. If a company reduces its dividend in order to finance a profitable internal project the share price may suffer if investors view the cut as a reflection of management's view of future prospects. This may happen where it has been common practice for a business to set the dividend at a level which is not sustainable in the future.

Many investors expect a certain dividend policy and invest in a business either to receive a regular income (dividend) or capital growth, depending on their personal circumstances. If the dividends were reduced or increased these investors would not receive the required form of return. Taxation, particularly for higher-rate tax payers, significantly affects an investor's dividend requirement. Higher-rate tax payers prefer capital appreciation to dividends, which are currently taxed at a top marginal rate of 60 per cent.

The particular circumstances of a business will determine the appropriate dividend policy, but many businesses aim for a steady growth in dividends as their objective.

Government Assistance

Central and local government assistance to business takes many forms and a complete review of such assistance is outside the scope of this book. It should be noted, however, that qualifying conditions and availability of assistance is liable to change at very short notice. A comprehensive review of government assistance can be found in *Finance for New Projects in the UK* published by Peat Marwick McLintock.

Outlined below are some of the grants available for financing new investments. There are two categories of such grants, those available nationally and those restricted to certain parts of the country.

Grants for major projects

Grants for major projects are available throughout the UK and are aimed at encouraging investments which will, through improved performance, yield significant benefits to the economy.

New investments should amount to at least £0.5 million, including additional working capital and ancillary costs directly associated with the project. Projects must be commercially viable and be forecast to result in a significant improvements in performance, introduce a substantial new benefit to UK output, or introduce a significant degree of innovation.

The terms of the grant are subject to individual negotiation. Assistance will normally be set at the minimum necessary to bring about the additional benefits associated with the project and is likely to be in the form of a cash grant. Account is taken of the nature and scale of the investment, the degree of risk, projected returns and industrial policy advantages.

Small firms finance

In suitable cases, the government may assist small businesses to raise finance through its Loan Guarantee Scheme.

Sole traders, partnerships, cooperatives or limited companies located anywhere in the UK are eligible, although there is a wide range of excluded activities. They may already be trading or they may be starting in business. There is no formal limitation on the numbers employed, turnover or assets, but applications will not be considered from large businesses or their subsidiaries.

Personal guarantees are not required under the scheme, but applicants must be prepared to pledge all available assets used or available for use in connection with the business as security for guaranteed loans. The government guarantees the repayment of 70 per cent of the medium-term loans (not overdrafts) made to the eligible businesses by the participating financial institutions.

In consideration for this guarantee the Department of Trade and Industry (DTI) charge a commercial premium 2.5 per cent payable quarterly on 70 per cent of the reducing balance of the amount guaranteed. Guaranteed loans may be for amounts of up to £75,000 prepayable over periods of between two and seven years.

Regional selective assistance

Selective financial assistance can be made available to

businesses in the assisted areas in the UK for manufacturing and service projects which have good prospects of viability, and which will improve or maintain employment prospects. Support is normally in the form of cash grants, including training grants, and is subject to individual negotiation with the DTI.

Regional Development Grants

The DTI makes regional development grants (RDGs) available for approved investment projects in certain development areas within the UK. In order for a project to qualify for RDGs, assets must be provided and/or jobs created; new or expanded capacity to produce goods or provide a service must be created; or a material change in the product or process must result; and it must relate to a qualifying activity.

Grants are calculated as being the higher of:

1. 15 per cent of eligible capital expenditure, subject to a maximum of £10,000 per job created.

2. £3,000 per job created, subject to a maximum of 40 per cent of initial investment in the case of manufacturing businesses.

Regional Loans from the European Community

The European Investment Bank (EIB) offers loans at favourable interest rates in the assisted areas. The EIB helps finance industrial project undertaken by the private sector, and infrastructure projects by the public sector. The loans represent a useful complement to any grants available in making up project finance.

Appendix

Useful Names and Addresses

Association of British Chambers of
Commerce,
212 Shaftesbury Avenue,
London WC2
Telephone 01–240 5831

BACS Limited,
De Havilland Road,
Edgware,
Middlesex HA8 5QA
Telephone 01–952 2333

British Export Houses Association,
69 Cannon Street,
London EC4N 5AB
Telephone: 01–248 4444

British Overseas Trade Board,
1 Victoria Street,
London SW1H 0ET
Telephone: 01–215 7877

Dun & Bradstreet Ltd.,
26–32 Clifton Street,
London EC2P 2LY
Telephone: 01-247 4377

Export Credits Guarantee
Department,
Aldermanbury House,
Aldermanbury,
London EC2P 2EL
Telephone: 01–606 6699

Institute of Credit Management,
Easton House,
Church Street,
Easton-on-the-Hill,
Stamford,
Lincolnshire PE9 3NZ
Telephone: (0780) 56777

Peat Marwick McLintock,
1 Puddle Dock,
Blackfriars,
London EC4V 3PD
Telephone: 01–236 8000

Registrar of Companies
Companies House,
Crown Way,
Maindy,
Cardiff CF4 3UZ
Telephone: (0222) 388588

Sterling Brokers Association,
Colechurch House,
1 London Bridge Walk,
London SE1 2SS
Telephone: 01–407 2767

The Stock Exchange,
London EC2N 1HP
Telephone: 01–588 2355

Index